SO, YOU THINK YOU KNOW THE SOUTH COAST?

FACTS, FOLKLORE, TRIVIA AND TREASURES

By Henry Quinlan
Photos by Caroline Murphy

Omni Publishing Co.
2021

Published by Omni Publishing Co.
www.omni-pub.com

Photography: Caroline E. Murphy
Cover Photographs: David Heath (Email: drh916@me.com)
Cover Design Consultant: David Derby

Library of Congress cataloging in publication data
Quinlan, Henry

So, You Think You Know the South Coast?
Facts, Folklore, Trivia and Treasures

ISBN: 978-1-928758-02-0

Preface

The term "South Coast" does not have a verifiable origin.

Todd Gross, a weatherman for WNEV-TV (the present-day WHDH-TV) in Boston, first used the phrase during the 1980s. Others say its origin dates back to a group of businessmen seeking to attract businesses.

The communities that make up the South Coast have remained arbitrary depending on who is describing them. For this book's purposes, the South Coast consists of the following communities: Wareham, Marion, Rochester, Mattapoisett, Fairhaven, New Bedford, Dartmouth, Fall River, and Westport.

I admit my knowledge was somewhat limited. Still, once I began to read and hear about the history, the remarkable people and experienced beautiful places, I wanted to learn more, and I did. I talked to many people seeking information and read many books. I note in the acknowledgment section those who were incredibly helpful. Everyone I asked was more than generous with their knowledge and time.

The book lays out a significant base knowledge for each community, including famous men and women who have made significant contributions to each community. A section, "Do You Know," brings forth some lesser-known information that contributes to the distinctness of each city or town. A photo section will test the reader's knowledge of buildings, views, and objects commonly seen but not necessarily recognized. There is a trivia chapter that will test the reader's knowledge about some well-known and lesser-known facts.

I note my "Treasures" of the South Coast. These are the institutions and places that make the South Coast a remarkable place to live and work. Some are cultural, some are natural, and some are historical, but each contributes to the quality of life available on the South Coast. The region and its people have something distinct and appealing to offer everyone.

Acknowledgement

I received a lot of help in putting this book together. Lou Pacheco, an old friend and former Chief of Staff to Mayor Sam Sutter of Fall River was invaluable in opening Fall River to me. My friend Bill Short a former New Bedford Banker offered insights into New Bedford and its economic history, Marion author Barbie Burr introduced me to the Marion Art Center, one of the "Treasures" of the South Coast and other delights of the South Coast. Others who contributed are Jodi Stevens, Executive Director Marion Art Center, Wendy Bidstrup, former Director of the Marion Art Center, Ken Pacheco of Fall River and Karsten Rathlev, noted tennis coach and director of The Marion Indoor Tennis Club, Luke and Barbara Easterly of Marion, Mike Hickey of Mattapoisett and Jackie Slade of Mattapoisett. Special thanks to Mary Jordan and Theresa Driscoll for their advice and editing skills.

Author Information

Henry M. Quinlan – *Grandfather*
Henry M. Quinlan, a graduate of Boston College and Suffolk University Law School, is a resident of Wareham, MA. He has been in the publishing business for 45 years and currently the owner and publisher of Omni Publishing Co.

Caroline E. Murphy – *Granddaughter*
Caroline E. Murphy is a resident of Mattapoisett, MA, and a graduate of Old Rochester Regional High School, where she was co-captain of the Track Team and the Soccer Team. She has completed two years of undergraduate work at Stonehill College. During the pandemic she is enrolled in Southern New Hampshire University taking online courses.

Publisher: Omni Publishing Co. www.omni-pub.com

Table of Contents

All About, Do You Know and Significant People

All About Acushnet

Acushnet is a town in Bristol County, Massachusetts. The population was 10,303 at the 2010 census.

Acushnet was first settled in 1659. It has been part of three separate towns throughout its history. It was formerly the northeastern section of Dartmouth, which included the towns of Westport, New Bedford, and Fairhaven. In 1787, New Bedford separated from Dartmouth and included the lands of Fairhaven and Acushnet. In 1812, Fairhaven was incorporated as a separate town, again including the lands of Acushnet. Finally, the town was officially incorporated in 1860. The name "Acushnet," which is also the name of the river the town lies on, comes from the Wampanoag *Cushnea*, meaning "peaceful resting place near water," originally designating the fact that the tribe which sold the land to the Puritans inhabited the lands leading up to the river.

In 1841, Herman Melville joined the crew of the whaler Acushnet. He later wrote about his travels at sea, culminating in the novel *Moby Dick*.

In 1910, the Acushnet Process Company (now the Acushnet Company) was founded in the town. The original Titleist golf ball was developed and produced in Acushnet. The Acushnet Company owns the Titleist brand name, under which golf balls, golf clubs, and other golf paraphernalia are manufactured and marketed.

Originally an agricultural community embracing the headwaters of the Acushnet River, the residential town of Acushnet has retained its rural atmosphere, while also providing a home for various industries. Through the 1800s, the town was the site of water-powered factories and boat yards; in the 1990s, the town hosted construction, manufacturing and agri/aquaculture industries. Acushnet is a quiet friendly community, with many miles of winding, country roads. Residents take great pride in the town's schools, openness, and feeling of family. Each fall, during the well-known Apple/Peach Festival, Acushnet's growers, artisans, and Historical Society welcome visitors from far and wide.

Acushnet Library

The town of Acushnet established a free library in 1896. The town's Russell Memorial Library, dedicated to a member of the prominent Russell family of New Bedford, lies in the town's population center. In fiscal year 2008, the town of Acushnet spent 0.87% ($189,813) of its budget on its public library—some $18 per person. On December 5, 2015, Russell Memorial Library closed its doors to relocate to the former Marie S. Howard School on Middle Road. The Acushnet Public Library opened on December 21, 2015.

Community Preservation Committee

The Community Preservation Act (CPA) is a smart growth tool that helps communities preserve open space and historic sites, create affordable housing, and develop outdoor recreational facilities. CPA also helps strengthen the state and local economies by expanding housing opportunities and construction jobs for the Commonwealth's workforce, and by supporting the tourism industry through preservation of the Commonwealth's historic and natural resources.

CPA allows communities to create a local Community Preservation Fund. Preservation monies are raised locally through the imposition of a surcharge of not more than 3 percent of the tax levy against real property, and municipalities must adopt CPA by ballot referendum

People of Significance – Acushnet

Gideon Nye (1812 – January 25, 1888) was an American diplomat, art collector, writer, and merchant in the East Indian and China trade, known both for his art collection and for his books on China. He was born in North Fairhaven, MA (now Acushnet), in 1812.

Nye went to China in 1831, where he worked for various companies in the East Indian and Chinese trade. In 1843, he opened the House of Nye, Parkin & Co. In 1851 the firm name changed its name to Nye Brothers & Co. and operated until 1856. In this period, it was also known as Bull, Nye, & Co. due to the brief involvement of Isaac Bull. Nye Brothers suffered a collapse in 1856 after over-investing during a down market.

Nye was a merchant in China for over fifty years and the American Vice Consul at Canton (now Guangzhou) for the last ten years of his life. He was a scholarly man with a reputation for integrity, active as a Vice President of the Medical Missionary Society, and a corresponding member of the American Geographical Society. He was known as one of Canton's oldest residents, having spent 55 years in that city since his arrival in 1831. He died in the city on January 25, 1888, and afterward, "the flags of the consulates, custom house and foreign ships in port were at half-mast two days in token of public esteem and sorrow."

Nye published many books and pamphlets as an eye-witness to the events which led up to the First Opium War, based on his acquaintance with Chinese people and foreigners living in China.

Clement Nye Swift was born in 1846 in Acushnet, Massachusetts, to Rhodolphus Nye Swift and Sylvia Hathaway. As a child, he attended the Friends Academy in Dartmouth, Massachusetts. His early interest was in painting animals, and he moved to France to study painting at the École des Beaux-Arts in Paris.

After the outbreak of the Franco-Prussian War in 1870, Swift moved to Brittany. He settled in the coastal town of Pont-Aven, where he joined the artistic community known as the Pont-Aven School. He lived there for ten years, and during this time, he produced the majority of his paintings. Between 1872 and 1880, he exhibited his work at the Paris Salon.

In 1881, Swift returned to Acushnet, Massachusetts, where he took up writing, producing a series of stories and poems. He married his cousin Annie Amelia Swift on October 15, 1895. He died March 29, 1918, and is buried in Acushnet Cemetery.

Do You Know – Achushnet?

In 1904, **Acushnet,** the little village to the north of Fairhaven, once an integral part of the larger township, was also having trouble with its educational responsibilities. It badly needed a new school, and the townspeople, with considerable hardship, had raised $1,000 toward the expense of construction, which was a near prohibitive $6,000. Henry Huttleston Rogers learned of the dilemma and sent $5,000, thus balancing out the indebtedness and making a new school for Acushnet a reality.

A year later, the **Methodist Society of Acushnet** received a $1,000 gift from Rogers to be applied to the building fund for the restoration of the church after a devastating fire.

The **Long Plain Friends Quaker Meetinghouse**, 1341 Main Street, Acushnet, is the only building on the National Historic Register in Acushnet. A serene setting in Acushnet, this structure, built-in 1759, has been restored and maintained. The Meetinghouse is available throughout the summer for interested parties looking to have a small wedding or reception or birthday parties.

The **Acushnet River** is the town line between it and New Bedford south of Main Street. There are several ponds in the town, including Hamlin's Mill Pond (along the Acushnet), East Pond, and a portion of Tinkham Pond, which lies along the Mattapoisett town line. The town lies within the coastal plain, mostly below 80 feet elevation, with higher points around Mendon and Perry Hills in the southeast of town and in the Sassaquin area in the northwest corner of town, where the highest point in town rises slightly above 160 feet above sea level. Most of the town's population lies along the New Bedford line, with the biggest area being in the southwest corner of the town, near the town hall.

The **Acushnet Public Schools** has wonderful a section on its website entitled "Extra Learning Resources." Available in this link are the following: Covid- 19 Resources, Home Learning Page, SSEA Home Videos, Library Links and Resources, Social/Emotional Supports and Boredom Busters, Virtual Field Trips, and Student Services.

The Acushnet Public School's website offers many varied resources. One of the most interesting are these links to virtual field trips.

Here are some direct links to Websites for virtual field trips:

Museum - National Gallery in Washington, DC
https://artsandculture.google.com/partner/national-gallery-of-art-washington-dc?hl=en

Rhode Island Museum of Science & Art
http://www.rimosa.org/

ZOO - San Diego
https://kids.sandiegozoo.org/

US STATES
https://kids.nationalgeographic.com/explore/states/

FARM - Pigs
https://www.farmfood360.ca/

Aquarium - Monterey
https://www.montereybayaquarium.org/animals/live-cams

All About Dartmouth

Dartmouth is a coastal town in Bristol County, Massachusetts. The Wampanoag inhabited the area that is now Dartmouth before European colonization. Bartholomew Gosnold first explored the area, which would later become Old Dartmouth, in 1602. Old Dartmouth, now the cities of New Bedford, Acushnet, Dartmouth, Fairhaven, and Westport, was purchased from the Wampanoag around March 7, 1652, for "30 yards of cloth, eight moose skins, fifteen axes, fifteen hoes, fifteen pair of breeches, eight blankets, two kettles, one cloak, £2 in wampum, eight pair stockings, eight pair shoes, one iron pot and 10 shillings in another commodity." Dartmouth was settled around November, 1662, and it was officially incorporated in 1664. Dartmouth's history was that of an agricultural and maritime community, but during the late 19th century, its coastline became a resort area for the wealthy members of New England society.

Old Dartmouth was the first area of Southeastern Massachusetts to be settled by Europeans. Dartmouth is part of New England's farm coast, consisting of a chain of historic coastal villages, vineyards, and farms. The official dog of Dartmouth is a Golden Retriever.

The northern part of Dartmouth contains the town's large commercial districts. The southern part of town abuts Buzzards Bay, and there are several other waterways, including Lake Noquochoke, Cornell Pond, Slocums River, Shingle Island River, and Paskamansett River. There are several working farms in town and one vineyard, which is part of the Coastal Wine Tour. The town also has a thriving agricultural heritage, and many of the working farms are protected. The town's food staple is French toast casserole.

The southern part of Dartmouth borders Buzzards Bay, where a lively fishing and boating community thrives; off its coast, the Elizabeth Islands and Cuttyhunk can be seen. The New Bedford Yacht Club in Padanaram hosts a bi-annual Regatta. With unique historic villages and a selection of coastal real estate, it has for many generations been a summering community. Notable affluent sections within South Dartmouth are Nonquitt, Round Hill, Barney's Joy, and Mishaum Point.

Dartmouth is the third largest town in Massachusetts, after Plymouth and Middleborough. Dartmouth's northernmost border with Freetown to Buzzards Bay in the south is approximately 16 miles.

The villages of Hixville, Bliss Corner, Padanaram, Smith Mills, and Russells Mills are located within the town.

Edward Howland Robinson Green, known as "Colonel" Ned Green, the only son of the renowned female tycoon and miser, Hetty Green, built his home on Round Hill after his mother's death in 1916. She left him and his sister a fortune of between $100 and $200 million. In 1948, twelve years after the Colonel's death, his sister Sylvia Green donated the entire property to the Massachusetts Institute of Technology, which used the 240-acre estate for educational and military purposes until 1964. In 1964, MIT sold the estate to the Society of Jesus of New England, which adapted the mansion as a religious retreat center. Currently it is privately owned by multiple owners.

Dartmouth is home to The University of Massachusetts Dartmouth, a public university. It is one of five campuses and operating subdivisions of the University of Massachusetts. Formerly Southeastern Massachusetts University, it was merged into the University of Massachusetts system in 1991.

The campus has an overall student body of 8,513 students (school year 2019–2020), including 6,841 undergraduates and 1,672 graduate students. As of the 2019–2020 academic year, UMass Dartmouth had 402 full-time faculty on staff. The university also includes the University of Massachusetts School of Law. It is classified among "R2: Doctoral Universities – High research activity."

People of Significance – Dartmouth

Naseer H. Aruri was an American scholar-activist and expert on Middle East politics, U.S. foreign policy in the Middle East, and human rights. Aruri was Chancellor Professor (Emeritus) of Political Science, having served on the faculty of the University of Massachusetts at Dartmouth from 1965-1998. In 1993, he was the recipient of the College of Arts and Sciences "Distinguished Research Award." Aruri's papers have been preserved and are on display at the Claire T. Carney Library Archives and Special Collections at UMass-Dartmouth. He was born on January 7, 1934, and died February 10, 2015.

Philip Henry Sheridan (March 6, 1831 – August 5, 1888) was a career United States Army officer and a Union general in the American Civil War. His career was noted for his rapid rise to major general and his close association with General-in-Chief Ulysses S. Grant. He transferred Sheridan from command of an infantry division in the Western Theater to lead the Cavalry Corps of the Army of the Potomac in the East. In 1864, he defeated Confederate forces under General Jubal Early in the Shenandoah Valley. His destruction of the economic infrastructure of the Valley, called "The Burning" by residents, was one of the first uses of scorched-earth tactics in the war. In 1865, his cavalry pursued Gen. Robert E. Lee and was instrumental in forcing his surrender at Appomattox.

Sheridan fought in later years in the Indian Wars of the Great Plains. Both as a soldier and private citizen, he was instrumental in the development and protection of Yellowstone National Park. In 1883, Sheridan was appointed General-in-Chief of the U.S. Army, and in 1888, he was promoted to the rank of General of the Army during the term of President Grover Cleveland.

In 1888 Sheridan suffered a series of massive heart attacks two months after sending his memoirs to the publisher. Although slender in his youth, by 57 years of age, he weighed over 200 pounds. After his first heart attack, the U.S. Congress quickly passed legislation to promote him to general of the Army on June 1, 1888. He received the news from a congressional delegation with joy, despite his pain. His family moved him from the heat of Washington to his summer cottage in the Nonquitt enclave of Dartmouth, where he died of heart failure on August 5, 1888.

Edith Ellen Greenwood was born in 1920 in North Dartmouth, to Ellen E. (Pearson) and Frederick James Greenwood. She attended St. Luke's Hospital School of Nursing in New Bedford, Massachusetts, and graduated in 1941. She served as a Lieutenant with the United States Army Nurse Corps (ANC) during World War II. She was the first female recipient of the Soldier's Medal, an award she received for saving 15 patients.

Téa Leoni, born **Elizabeth Pantaleoni,** February 25, 1966, is an American actress and producer. In her early career, she starred in the television sitcoms *Flying Blind* (1992–93) and *The Naked Truth* (1995–98). Her breakthrough role was in the 1995 action comedy film *Bad Boys*. In later years, Leoni had lead roles in films such as *Deep Impact* (1998), *The Family Man* (2000), *Jurassic Park III* (2001), *Spanglish* (2004), *and Fun with Dick and Jane* (2005). In 2014, she returned to television in the leading role of the CBS political drama series *Madam Secretary*. Her parents lived in Dartmouth.

Lewis Lee Millett Sr. (December 15, 1920 – November 14, 2009) was a U.S. Army officer who received the Medal of Honor during the Korean War for leading the last significant American bayonet charge. He enlisted in the U.S. National Guard while still in high school and in 1940 joined the U.S. Army Air Corps. When he thought the U.S. would not participate in World War II, he deserted and went to Canada with a friend where they joined the Canadian Army and were sent to London. The U.S. did enter the war, and by the time he made it to Europe, they were in the fight, so he transferred to the U.S. Army. While serving in WW II, he received a Silver Star for driving a burning ammunition truck away from a group of soldiers before it exploded.

During the Korean War, Millett was awarded the United States military's highest decoration, the Medal of Honor. The citation explains that he successfully led a bayonet charge against the enemy. He later served in the Vietnam War as well. He retired from the Army in 1973 and died of congestive heart failure in 2009. Millett grew up in South Dartmouth and graduated from Dartmouth High School.

Do You Know – Dartmouth?

Volunteers are needed for all aspects of food production at the community farm, **Harvest Farm**. All produce is donated to the Hunger Commission. In the first seven seasons, Sharing the Harvest grew and donated more than 143,000 pounds of food and hosted more than 10,000 volunteers. Volunteer drop-in hours are held from 9 a.m. to noon and 2-5 p.m. Monday, Tuesday, Wednesday, and Saturday 9 a.m. to noon.

The village of **Padanaram** was one of many settlements that began cropping up within the town of Old Dartmouth after its purchase from the Wampanoag by members of the Plymouth Colony in 1652. During King Philip's War, the settlement was burned down, and all cattle were killed. The only settlers who survived were those who heard a warning and fled either to Russell's Garrison or Cooke's Garrison. Remains of the settlement can still be seen at the foot of Lucy Street.

The name "Padanaram" came from a prominent early resident named Laban Thatcher, who identified with the Biblical figure Laban who resided in Paddan Aram in Mesopotamia. The village eventually adopted this new name and dropped its earlier Wampanoag name, "Ponagansett."

The **New Bedford Yacht Club** in Padanaram, South Dartmouth, was founded in New Bedford. NBYC bi-annually hosts the Buzzards Bay Regatta. Its Sailing School for children and adults is open to members and non-members alike.

The **Old Dartmouth Historical Society** — long a proud asset of the New Bedford area — was incorporated in 1903 and forced to lease the Masonic Building as a meeting place. For want of funds to buy adequate meeting quarters, this arrangement lasted for three years.

In September of 1906, a meeting of the organization was held in the vacated Bank of Commerce Building. It was announced that this building had been purchased as an anonymous gift to the old Dartmouth Historical Society. It was not until 1909 at the death of Henry H. Rogers that the information was revealed, naming Mr. Rogers as the generous donor. The building is still a segment of the Society's complex in New Bedford's Historic District.

Conveniently located just across from the Slocum's River Reserve canoe launch, **Upper Cedar Island and Lower Cedar Island** are a great place to start a Slocum's River paddling adventure. The Dartmouth Natural Resources Trust (DNRT) preserved these two islands for their exceptional salt marsh and bird habitat. During the summer, you may spot a pair of osprey nesting on the tall platform on Lower Cedar and hunting over the river. Because both islands are mostly salt marsh, they're better discovered from the water than by foot.

Running Brook Vineyard and Winery was founded in 1998 in Dartmouth by Pedro Teixeira and Manuel Morais out of a vision to produce top quality wines that will make New Englanders proud and satisfy their palates. Since the founding, the winery has grown and sells its wines in its Dartmouth & Westport vineyards.

Edward Howland Robinson Green, known as "Colonel" Ned Green, the only son of the renowned female tycoon and miser, Hetty Green, built his home on Round Hill after his mother's death in 1916 left him and his sister with a fortune of between $100 and $200 million.

In 1948, twelve years after the Colonel's death, his sister Sylvia Green, his heir, donated the entire property to the Massachusetts Institute of Technology (MIT), which used the 240-acre estate for educational and military purposes until 1964. In 1964, MIT sold the estate to the Society of Jesus of New England. It adapted the mansion as a religious retreat center. In 1968, the Jesuits sold much of the estate's beach to the Town of Dartmouth, and in 1970, it sold the entire property to Gratia R. Montgomery, a local woman. In 1981, she sold most of the site to private developers, who developed it as a private, gated condominium community.

Contrary to the popular notion that influential **Quaker merchants** of old Dartmouth would not tolerate local ships being outfitted as privateers because of their pacifist convictions, more than one Dartmouth "fighting Quaker" was among the owners and shareholders of 11 privateering vessels that operated during the Revolutionary War listed in Beverly Glennon's local history, Dartmouth: The Early History of a Massachusetts Coastal Town.

All About Fairhaven

Fairhaven is a town in Bristol County, Massachusetts. It is located on the South Coast, where the Acushnet River flows into Buzzards Bay, an arm of the Atlantic Ocean. The town shares a harbor with New Bedford, a place well-known for its whaling and fishing heritage; consequently, Fairhaven's history, economy, and culture are closely aligned with those of its larger neighbor. The population of Fairhaven was 15,873 at the time of the 2010 census.

Fairhaven was first settled in 1659 as "Cushnea," the easternmost part of Dartmouth. It was founded on land purchased by English settlers at the Plymouth Colony from the Wampanoag sachem Massasoit, and his son, Wamsutta.

In 1787, the eastern portion of Dartmouth seceded and formed a new settlement called New Bedford. This new town included the present-day towns of Fairhaven, Acushnet, and New Bedford itself. Fairhaven eventually separated from New Bedford, and it was officially incorporated in 1812. At that time, Fairhaven included all of the lands on the east bank of the Acushnet River. The northern portion of Fairhaven, upriver from Buzzards Bay, formed another independent town, called Acushnet, in 1860. Thus, what had once been a single town, Dartmouth, with a substantial land area, became, in less than 75 years, four separate municipalities. The western portion of the original Dartmouth land-purchase eventually became a fifth town, Westport.

Fairhaven was also a whaling port; in the year 1838, Fairhaven was the second-largest whaling port in the United States, with 24 vessels sailing for the whaling grounds. The author of Moby-Dick, Herman Melville, departed from the port of Fairhaven aboard the whaleship Acushnet in 1841.

According to the United States Census Bureau, the town has a total area of 14.1 square miles, of which 12.4 square miles is land and 1.7 square miles or 12.06%, is water. Fort Phoenix (now the Fort Phoenix

19

State Reservation) is located in Fairhaven at the mouth of the Acushnet River, and it served, during colonial and revolutionary times, as the primary defense against seaborne attacks on New Bedford harbor.

Within sight of the fort, the first naval battle of the American Revolution took place on May 14, 1775. Under the command of Nathaniel Pope and Daniel Egery, a group of 25 Fairhaven minutemen (including Noah Stoddard) aboard the sloop *Success* retrieved two vessels previously captured by a British warship in Buzzards Bay.

In the town are several distinctive public buildings that were donated by Henry Huttleston Rogers and his family. One of the them is the public library, The Millicent Library, named after the daughter of Henry Rogers.

Construction started in 1891 on the chosen site, in the style of Italian Renaissance; it was completed in 1892. Charles Brigham, foremost American architect of his day from the Boston firm of Brigham & Spofford, was chosen to draw the plans. Norcross Brothers, the richest building firm in the country, was given orders to use the best of everything — no defaced or discolored materials to be tolerated; and there was to be particular emphasis on the artistic in every phase of planning. Arthur Robinson, expert painter and finisher of fine woods, had charge of all painting, rubbing and staining.

The basement segment of the walls was made of granite from Norcross Brothers' Branbury quarries; the remainder of the building was constructed of Dedham granite, rock-faced. Ornamentation was effected by beautifully fashioned terra cotta wreaths and garlands in a luminous golden hue, while the roofs were tiled in deep red; gutters, conductors, finials and ridge rolls were of copper.

Within the building, there were sheathing, doors and door casings of heavy oak, beautifully grained. Masterly carving of some of this magnificent wood was spectacular. Much of the inside wall area was finished in fine brick stenciled to a rich and intricate pattern. There were Perth Amboy fireplaces throughout. And opposite Millicent's window, the roof flared to a domed loftiness providing height for later adjustment of book galleries as need might demand.

The reading room to the right of the main entrance also swept to a dramatic dome broken by a semi-circular curve of lofty window apertures providing excellent natural lighting. Stained glass gleamed in panels over doorways, and a spectacular oriel window in the librarian's room shimmered in muted color.

In the Millicent Library, there is a spectacular window of stained glass. It is sixteen feet in height and was crafted in 1891 in London by the firm of Clayton & Bell. Within one of its compartments is depicted in gem-like colors a likeness of the great Shakespeare. To right and left in encircling frames are the names of American poets, but the lower and outstanding pane shows a female form — the gentle muse of poetry herself in softly draped robes — her face, pure and lovely, raised in a sort of adoration. The spectator knows at once that this is a real face, the actual likeness of a flesh and blood maiden. The face is that of Millicent G. Rogers, in whose memory the window was mounted — and, indeed, the whole building was raised.

Fairhaven High School and Academy is a public high school in Fairhaven, Massachusetts. Its main building, built in 1905, is known as the "Castle on the Hill" and it is part of the Fairhaven Public Schools district. The school was voted the "most beautiful high school in Massachusetts" in 2017.

The school building was added to the National Register of Historic Places in 1981. The building was donated in 1906 by Henry Huttleston Rogers, who was one of the key men in John D. Rockefeller's Standard Oil Trust.

Other buildings in Fairhaven donated by Henry Rogers are the Rogers School, the Town Hall and Unitarian Memorial Church. A granite shaft on the High School lawn is dedicated to Rogers. In Riverside Cemetery, the Henry Huttleston Rogers Mausoleum is patterned after the Temple of Minerva in Athens, Greece. Henry, his first wife Abbie, and several family members are interred there.

People of Significance – Fairhaven

Henry Huttleston Rogers (1840–1909). One of the key men in the Standard Oil Trust, Rogers was one of the last of the Gilded Age robber barons in the United States. He was also a "secret" philanthropist. A descendant of the original Mayflower Pilgrims, he made his fortune in the oil refining business, becoming a leader at Standard Oil. He also played a significant role in numerous corporations and business enterprises in the gas, copper, and railroad industries. Rogers and his wife, Abbie Gifford Rogers, another Fairhaven native (who was the daughter of the whaling captain Peleg Gifford), donated many community improvements in the late-nineteenth- and early-twentieth-century. Among the donations are a grammar school, an extraordinarily luxurious high school, the Town Hall, the George H. Taber Masonic Building, the Unitarian Memorial Church, the Tabitha Inn, the Millicent Library, and a modern water-and-sewer system. These structures were erected to top-quality construction standards, a trademark philosophy of Henry H. Rogers; most are still in regular use more than one hundred years later.

Nakahama "John" Manjirō. In 1843, Fairhaven became the home of the first Japanese person to live in America, "John" Manjiro Nakahama (1827–1898). The ties of friendship, first formed when a Fairhaven whaling captain rescued fourteen-year-old Manjiro Nakahama from a small island in the Pacific Ocean, have endured to this day and make Fairhaven a popular spot for visitors from Japan. Upon returning to Japan in 1846, Manjiro was imprisoned because Japan forbade its people from leaving. However, his familiarity with American customs and the English language became important when Commodore Matthew C. Perry first arrived to open Japan to trade relations with the western world. Manjiro rose to prominence in Japanese governmental circles and was made a samurai. He promoted the acceptance of American ideas and technology. He has also been credited with introducing the necktie to Japan.

Joshua Slocum was born in 1844 in Mount Hanley, Nova Scotia. At 14 years of age, he ran away from home and signed on as a cabin boy on a fishing boat. Slocum returned after a brief time but left home for good at the age of 16 and signed on to a merchant ship as an ordinary seaman. In 1865, he settled in San Francisco, became an American citizen, continued life at sea, and became a Master. At the end of 1867, Slocum found himself, his wife, and son stranded in Brazil after his uninsured vessel ran aground. At this point, he and his family built a boat from scrap, the Liberdade, and sailed it to Washington DC. He wrote a self-published a book, which did not do well. He moved to Boston and began working in a Boston shipyard.

In 1892, an acquaintance gave Slocum an old sloop, the *Spray*, which was located in Fairhaven. He and his family spent 13 months in Fairhaven completely rebuilding the *Spray*, a 36-foot, 9inch gaff-rigged sloop oyster boat. Just as he did in Brazil, he used discarded material to rebuild. Upon completion in 1894, it was used for an unsuccessful fishing expedition. Slocum was middle-aged and groping for a living; the world saw no value in his sailing skills.

He then decided to sail around the world, solo, in the *Spray*. On April 24, 1895, he left Boston and ended his journey in Newport, RI, on June 27, 1898, after sailing 46,000 miles. It was the first solo circumnavigation of the world.

Slocum wrote a book about his adventures, *Sailing Alone Around the World*. With income from the book, he retired to Martha's Vineyard. Land life was not for him, and he returned to the sea in the *Spray*.

On September 14, 1919, he set sail from Massachusetts and was never heard from again. He never learned to swim as he considered it useless.

Today the student newspaper at Fairhaven High School is named the "Spray."

William Nye, in 1840 at the age of sixteen, left his family on Cape Cod on a journey that took him to California's gold rush and into the Civil War as a Unionist soldier.

In 1855, Nye returned to New Bedford and set up an oil and kerosene business. He operated until the outbreak of the American Civil War

23

when he joined the Union Army as a sutler to the Massachusetts Artillery and the 4th Massachusetts Cavalry. Nye was with the advance guard of the cavalry when it entered Richmond, Virginia, in 1865, and set up a trading post there in one of the city's remaining brick buildings. For a time, he was the sole tradesman operating in Richmond. After his regiment was mustered out in November, 1865, Nye returned to New Bedford and began developing the lubricant oil business for which he became principally known.

Nye's oil business, initially run out of small rented premises in Fairhaven, focused primarily on highly refined lubricant oils for watches, clocks, typewriters, sewing machines, and bicycles. In the late 1860s, he acquired an entire catch of 2,200 pilot whales, which would supply the raw material for his lubricating oils for several years. He expanded the business in 1877 by purchasing a large brick building on Fish Island, which became its principal refinery. By 1888, his company had become one of the world's largest suppliers of refined lubricant oils. In 1896 Nye absorbed Ezra Kelley's oil company, his main rival. He remained actively involved in the business until shortly before his death in 1910 at 86.

The business exists today in Fairhaven as Nye Lubricants.

Mary Ann Tripp (nee Hathaway) was the first American woman to visit China and the first American woman to circumnavigate the earth. She also visited the Philippine Islands during this historic trip. She then went on to travel the globe and visit China two more times before settling into a long life in Fairhaven, Massachusetts.

Do You Know – Fairhaven?

There is a farm located in Fairhaven, Massachusetts that supports a herd of all-natural, grass-fed **Angus cattle**. The farm, which is approximately 500 acres, is situated on Shaw's Cove Rd. The fields grow all of the grass and corn that support the herd of 100 all-natural, grass-fed Black Angus cattle.

Though it extends far out into the waters of Buzzards Bay, **West Island** is the only island on this list you can get to without a boat! West Island was connected to the mainland by a causeway in the 1940s, and more than half of this charming island is protected as West Island State Reservation and West Island Town Beach. Hike, swim, snorkel, dig for quahogs or relax on salt marsh-lined beaches at this unique spot.

Fairhaven's **Little Bay** has an array of islands that make for a fantastic day of kayak exploration. It is recommended to launch from Edgewater Street and heading north to circle the extensive salt marsh island across from Little Bay Conservation Area, known as Quahog Hill. The Buzzards Bay Coalition protected this island in 2014, making it a great place to spot wildlife; be sure not to tread on or disturb marsh vegetation. From Quahog Hill, head south to loop around a picturesque, crescent-shaped island in the South Shore Marshes Wildlife Management Area (WMA) and stop for a picnic on the white sand beaches of the WMA's long salt marsh peninsula. As you head back to shore, you'll pass by a privately-owned island off the end of Wampanoag Drive, where the public is not permitted.

Fort Phoenix (now the Fort Phoenix State Reservation) is located in Fairhaven at the mouth of the Acushnet River. During colonial and revolutionary times, the fort was the primary defense against seaborne attacks on New Bedford harbor.

The first naval battle of the American Revolution took place on May 14, 1775. Under the command of Nathaniel Pope and Daniel Egery, a group of 25 Fairhaven minutemen (including Noah Stoddard) aboard the sloop Success retrieved two vessels previously captured by a British warship in Buzzards Bay.

The fort was enlarged before the War of 1812, and it helped repel an attack on the harbor by British forces. In the early morning hours of June 13, 1814, landing boats were launched from the British raider, HMS Nimrod. Alerted by the firing of the guns at Fort Phoenix, the militia gathered, and the British did not come ashore.

The fort was decommissioned in 1876, and in 1926 the site was donated to the town by Cara Rogers Broughton (a daughter of Henry Huttleston Rogers). Today, the area surrounding the fort includes a park and a bathing beach. The fort lies just to the seaward side of the harbor's hurricane barrier.

In 1838, **Fairhaven** was the second-largest whaling port in the United States, with 24 vessels sailing for the whaling grounds. Fairhaven's economy evolved into one that supplemented the New Bedford economy rather than competing directly with it. Fairhaven became a town of shipwrights, ship chandlers, rope makers, coopers, and sailmakers. It also became a popular location for ship-owners and ship-captains to build their homes and raise their children.

The **friends of Henry Huttleston Rogers** were Booker T. Washington, Anne Sullivan, Helen Keller, and Mark Twain, who came to visit Rogers in Fairhaven, sometimes for protracted periods.

Fairhaven is home to two **internationally known companies;** Fairhaven is the home of the Acushnet Company, a world-renowned manufacturer of golf equipment, balls, and apparel. Fairhaven is also home to Nye Lubricants, a firm dealing in industrial lubricants and whose history dates back to 1844.

The school's teams are known as the **Blue Devils**, and their colors are royal blue and white. The school's fight song is sung to the tune of the "Notre Dame Fight Song."

Kanawha was a 471-ton steam-powered luxury yacht built in 1899 for millionaire industrialist and financier **Henry Huttleston Rogers** (1840–1909). One of the key men in the Standard Oil Trust, Rogers, was one of the last of the robber barons of the Gilded Age in the United States. It required a crew of 39 men to operate it.

Henry Huttleston Rogers was also a **"secret" philanthropist**." All this philanthropy is well remembered because it is so apparent, but it has been forgotten that Mr. Rogers' magnanimity did not stop at the boundaries of his town. His concern embraced the entire area. Since he was loath to make public his donations — the extent of his charity to this whole of the community was not realized until after his death — and even now, much of his quiet goodness can only be surmised.

A year **after Rogers' death**, Z.W. Pease of the *New Bedford Standard* editorial staff, writing an article in the *Boston Sunday Globe* stated:

"It was the habit of the late Henry H. Rogers in his lifetime to send at Christmas time — a handsome donation for practically every New Bedford charity. Many societies received a fixed contribution of $750 annually, and their work was based upon an income of which this was a considerable part. Now that the income is no longer forthcoming, one after another is making a public appeal for funds to make up deficiencies."

In 1901 — during an epidemic of typhoid fever, facilities of this new hospital were incredibly strained. A friend (later discovered to be H.H. Rogers) contributed $40,000 for a new ward for private patients, thereby expanding patient capacity by twenty beds. This ward was built from plans by a Boston architect, George H. Ingraham, and was erected in red brick with end porches. Rogers also contributed $1,000 for beds and $4,000 to defray other extras.

Mr. Rogers' concern for the women on the nursing staff became evident when he anonymously volunteered $1,000 toward establishing a nurses' ward. Although the working conditions of the nurses had significantly improved after the erection of the Page Street edifices — the young women in an ever-expanding training program needed space, privacy, and more home-like accommodations.

In 1904-05, a friend purchased a lot of land north of the hospital extending to Taber Street and containing 267.74 rods. It was announced that this friend would erect a nurses' home at a contemplated expense of $75,000. During this same period, Mr. Rogers was building just across the river — the imposing Fairhaven High School opened in 1906. So the two gracious buildings rose simultaneously, and on May 1, 1907, **Saint Luke's nurses** occupied the White Home.

The building offered accommodations for forty-four nurses. It was constructed of Harvard brick with pale trimming. A wide veranda supported by impressive white pillars stretched across the south front and relieved the austerity of a simply patterned Colonial design.

The **American Nail Company** was originally a Boston corporation organized in 1864. Still, in 1865, the business moved to Fairhaven and located in the Rodman buildings on Fort Street — a property that had once been the locale for the manufacturing of spermaceti candles. The company gradually diverted its manufacturing zeal to making of tacks, and the American Tack Company was organized through the consolidation of several small companies from Assonet, Taunton, and Dighton.

The absence of steady employment in an area recovering very slowly from the traumatic collapse of the whaling trade had, for some time, troubled Henry Rogers. He felt that his town must have a dependable industry and decided to lend impetus to the already-established tack-making business, which was exhibiting exceptional promise.

In 1899, at a mortgagee's sale, by a series of astute moves, he attained 25% of the Atlas Company's bonds for $200,000 — thus acquiring the property in Fairhaven, Taunton, Duxbury, and Plymouth. He determined to bring the assets and locale of the Atlas Tack Company to Fairhaven — and for that purpose commenced the erection of a complete and modern factory on South Pleasant Street. In April 1902, a thousand people attended the dedication ball held in the mammoth plant.

Rogers had been warned that if he insisted on locating in Fairhaven, transportation and accessibility of raw materials would be a problem. He was advised to locate in New York. This advice went unheeded, and he declared, "It is Fairhaven or no-where!"

Five hundred persons were eventually employed there, making tacks, eyelets, rivets, and certain types of nails. The plant employed not only Fairhaven people but numbers from surrounding and far-flung areas. At one time, about 10% of all the tackers in the country found employment there, for tack-making was skilled work requiring long apprenticeship and commensurate high wages.

The **Atlas Tack Company** is the only corporation in which Mr. Rogers is interested, which was not conducted for the purpose of making money!

"It is a well-known fact here that the plant is being operated at a loss to the owner, but he has continued its operation as a matter of civic pride and for the public welfare rather than for personal gain."

The Atlas Tack Corporation has been a first-rate asset to the area for many years. It must have cost Rogers millions to maintain during the difficult period of its birthing. The whole experiment shows remarkable vision and illustrates the Rogers' belief that man must have work to keep him healthy and self-respecting.

Perhaps it would be fitting, then, to end this revelation of quiet beneficence as we began it — with yet another Biblical reference. In Matthew 5:15, we read:

"Neither do men light a candle, and put it under a bushel, but on a candlestick; that it giveth light unto all that are in the house."

The Phoenix Bike Trail with its flat, paved path through 4.5 miles of Fairhaven's forests, salt marshes, and neighborhoods, the Phoenix Bike Trail is a safe and beautiful place for local bicyclists, runners, and walkers to explore. Whether on wheels or on foot, discover this town-managed bike path, which is part of the regional South Coast Bikeway.

There is a small secluded beach on West Island that can be found by using the trail map on All Trails. The trailhead is located on Fir Street in Fairhaven. This is a residential area with limited parking. There is a kiosk to mark the trailhead. Follow what looks like an old road for almost a mile until you get to the bay. From there follow a sandy trail to the right and you will come upon a beautiful secluded beach.

The **Old Stone Schoolhouse** was built in the Oxford Village neighborhood in 1828. It was the first school built under the school district system. Restored in the 1870s the schoolhouse is open on Saturdays in June, July, and August to teach about New England school days of long ago. It is also available for school trips.

Francis Ford Seymour, wife of actor Henry Fonda and mother of actors Peter and Jane Fonda, lived on Green Street for several years and graduated from Fairhaven High School in 1925. The Seymours were in Fairhaven from 1922 to 1936 and may have come here through connections with the family of Henry H. Rogers. Francis' father Eugene Seymour was the uncle of Mary Benjamin, who married Henry H. Rogers, Jr.

Northeast Maritime Institute is a private, co-educational institution that offers its students an opportunity to pursue maritime career-oriented education. Northeast Maritime Institute began in 1981 as a New England branch of the Tidewater School of Navigation based in Norfolk, Virginia. In 1995, Eric Dawicki, USMM Third Mate and Ship Management Consultant, and Angela Dawicki took ownership of Northeast Maritime. In 1996, the school changed its name to Northeast Maritime Institute (NMI) and relocated to New Bedford.

In 2001 the Institute moved to Fairhaven, into an award winning restored historic Federal style building located at 32 Washington Street.

In the last thirty years, Northeast Maritime Institute has grown into one of the largest privately held maritime education facilities in the United States. The institute has educated thousands of mariner students at all levels of U.S. Coast Guard licenses and documentation.

Martha Simon was the last of the Native Americans in Fairhaven. She was a Wampanoag. She was the subject in a painting erroneously entitled, "The Last of the Narragansetts." It is on display at the Millicent Library. This painting is by Albert Bierstadt – a departure for him from the panoramic landscapes of the West for which he is best known. He presented the painting to Henry Huttleston Rogers, in the hopes of currying favor as inventor of a device for a railway car (Henry Rogers owned a railroad,) although in the letter accompanying the painting, Bierstadt says "I cannot afford to waste my time making money."

Martha Simon was a respected member of the community.

All About Fall River

Fall River is a city in Bristol County, Massachusetts, The City of Fall River's population was 88,857 at the 2010 census, making it the tenth-largest city in the state. Located along the eastern shore of Mount Hope Bay at the mouth of the Taunton River, the city became famous during the 19th century as the leading textile manufacturing center in the United States. While the textile industry has long since moved on, its impact on the city's culture and landscape remains to this day. Fall River's official motto is "We'll Try", dating back to the aftermath of the Great Fire of 1843. It is also nicknamed the "Scholarship City" because Irving Fradkin founded Dollars for Scholars there in 1958. In 2017, Mayor Jasiel Correia introduced the "Make It Here" slogan as part of a citywide rebranding effort.

Fall River is known for the Lizzie Borden case, Portuguese culture, its numerous 19th-century textile mills and Battleship Cove, the world's largest collection of World War II naval vessels and the home of the battleship USS Massachusetts. Fall River is also the only city in the United States to have its city hall located over an interstate highway, Interstate 195 (Rhode Island-Massachusetts).

At the time of the establishment of the Plymouth Colony in 1620, the area that would one day become Troy City was inhabited by the Pokanoket Wampanoag tribe, headquartered at Mount Hope in what is now Bristol, Rhode Island. The "falling" river that the name Fall River refers to is the Quequechan River (pronounced "quick-a-shan" by locals) which flows through the city, dropping steeply into the bay. Quequechan is a Wampanoag word believed to mean "falling river" or "leaping/falling waters."

In 1653, Freetown was settled at Assonet Bay by members of the Plymouth Colony, as part of Freeman's Purchase, which included the northern part of what is now Fall River. In 1683, Freetown was incorporated as a town within the colony. The southern part of what is now Fall

River was incorporated as the town of Tiverton as part of the Massachu-setts Bay Colony in 1694, a few years after the merger with Plymouth Colony. In 1746, in the settlement of a colonial boundary dispute be-tween Rhode Island and Massachusetts, Tiverton was annexed to Rhode Island, along with Little Compton and what is now Newport County, Rhode Island. The boundary was then placed approximately at what is now Columbia Street.

In 1703, Benjamin Church, a hero of King Philip's War established a saw mill, grist mill, and a fulling mill on the Quequechan River. In 1714, Church sold his land, along with the water rights to Richard Bor-den of Tiverton and his brother Joseph. This transaction would prove to be extremely valuable 100 years later, helping to establish the Borden family as the leaders in the development of Fall River's textile industry.

In 1803, Fall River was separated from Freetown and officially in-corporated as its own town. A year later, Fall River changed its name to "Troy." The name "Troy" was used for 30 years and was officially changed back to Fall River on February 12, 1834. During this period, Fall River was governed by a three-member Board of Selectmen, until it became a City in 1854.

In 1835, The Fall River Female Anti-Slavery Society was formed (one of the many anti-slavery societies in New England) to promote abo-lition and to allow a women's space to conduct social activism.

In July 1843, the first great fire in Fall River's history destroyed much of the town center, including the Athenaeum, which housed the Skeleton in Armor which had been discovered in a sand bank in 1832 near what is now the corner of Hartwell and Fifth Street.

During this time, the southern part of what is now Fall River (south of Columbia Street) would remain part of Tiverton, Rhode Island. In 1856, the town of Tiverton, Rhode Island voted to split off its industrial northern section as Fall River, Rhode Island. In 1861, after decades of dispute, the United States Supreme Court moved the state boundary to what is now State Avenue, unifying both Fall Rivers as a city in Massa-chusetts.

The early establishment of the textile industry in Fall River grew out of the developments made in nearby Rhode Island beginning with Samuel Slater at Pawtucket in 1793. In 1811, Col. Joseph Durfee, the

Revolutionary War veteran and hero of the Battle of Freetown in 1778 built the Globe Manufactory (a spinning mill) at the outlet of Cook Pond on Dwelly St. near what is now Globe Four Corners in the city's South End. (It was part of Tiverton, Rhode Island at the time.) While Durfee's mill was never very successful, it marked the beginning of the city's rise in the textile business.

The real development of Fall River's industry, however, would occur along the falling river from which it was named, about a mile north of Durfee's first mill. The Quequechan River, with its eight falls, combined to make Fall River the best tidewater privilege in southern New England. It was perfect for industrialization—big enough for profit and expansion, yet small enough to be developed by local capital without interference from Boston.

The Fall River Manufactory was established by David Anthony and others in 1813. That same year, the Troy Cotton & Woolen Manufactory was also founded, by a group of investors led by Oliver Chace, from Swansea, who had worked as a carpenter for Samuel Slater in his early years. The Troy Mill opened in 1814, at the upper end of the falls.

In 1821, Colonel Richard Borden established the Fall River Iron Works, along with Maj. Bradford Durfee at the lower part of the Quequechan River. Durfee was a shipwright, and Borden was the owner of a grist mill. After an uncertain start, in which some early investors pulled out, the Fall River Iron Works was incorporated in 1825. The Iron Works began producing nails, bar stock, and other items such as bands for casks in the nearby New Bedford whaling industry. They soon gained a reputation for producing nails of high quality, and business flourished. In 1827, Col. Borden began regular steamship service to Providence, Rhode Island.

The American Print Works was established in 1835 by Holder Borden, uncle of Colonel Richard. With the leadership of the Borden family, the American Print Works (later known as the American Printing Company) became the largest and most important textile company in the city, employing thousands at its peak in the early 20th century. Richard Borden also constructed the Metacomet Mill in 1847, which today is the oldest remaining textile (cloth-producing) mill in the city, located on Agawam Street.

By 1845, the Quequechan's power had been all but maximized. The Massasoit Steam Mill was established in 1846, above the dam near the end of Pleasant Street. However, it would be another decade or so when improvements in the steam engine by George Corliss would enable the construction of the first large steam-powered mill in the city, the Union Mills in 1859.

The advantage of being able to import bales of cotton and coal to fuel the steam engines to Fall River's deep water harbor, and ship out the finished goods also by water, made Fall River the choice of a series of cotton mill magnates. The first railroad line serving Fall River, The Fall River Branch Railroad, was incorporated in 1844 and opened in 1845. Two years later, in 1847, the first regular steamboat service to New York City began. The Fall River Line as it came to be known operated until 1937, and for many years, was the preferred way to travel between Boston and Manhattan. The Old Colony Railroad and Fall River Railroad merged in 1854, forming the Old Colony and Fall River Railroad.

In 1854, Fall River was officially incorporated as a city, and had a population of about 12,000. Its first mayor was James Buffington.

Fall River profited well from the American Civil War and was in a fine position to take advantage of the prosperity that followed. By 1868, it had surpassed Lowell as the leading textile city in America with over 500,000 spindles.

In 1871 and 1872, a "most dramatic expansion" of the city occurred: 15 new corporations were founded, building 22 new mills throughout the city, while some of the older mills expanded. The city's population increased by 20,000 people during these two years, while overall mill capacity doubled to more than 1,000,000 spindles.

By 1876, the city had one sixth of all New England cotton capacity and one half of all print cloth production. The "Spindle City" as it became known, was second in the world to only Manchester, England.

To house the thousands of new workers, mostly Irish and French Canadian immigrants during these years, thousands of units of company housing were built. Unlike the well-spaced boardinghouses of the tidy cottages of Rhode Island, worker housing in Fall River consisted of thousands of wood-framed multi-family tenements, usually three-floor "triple-deckers" with up to six apartments. Many more privately owned tenements supplemented the company housing.

During the 19th century, Fall River became famous for the granite rock on which much of the city is built. Several granite quarries operated during this time, the largest of which was the Beattie Granite Quarry, near what is now North Quarry Street, near the corner of Locust. Many of the mills in the city were built from this native stone, and it was highly regarded as a building material for many public buildings and private homes alike. The Chateau-sur-Mer mansion in Newport, Rhode Island is perhaps the best example of Fall River granite being used for private home construction.

While most of the mills "above the hill" were constructed from native Fall River granite, nearly all of their counterparts along the Taunton River and Mount Hope Bay were made of red brick. This was due to the high costs and impracticality associated with transporting the rock through the city and down the hill, where there were no rail lines because of the steep grades. One notable exception is the Sagamore Mills on North Main Street, which were constructed from similar rock quarried in Freetown and brought to the site by rail.

Fall River rode the wave of economic prosperity well into the early 20th century. During this time, the city boasted several fancy hotels, theaters, and a bustling downtown. As the city continually expanded during the late 19th century, its leaders built several fine parks, schools, streetcar lines, a public water supply, and sewerage system to meet the needs of its growing population. In 1920 the population of Fall River peaked at 120,485

The cotton mills of Fall River had built their business largely on one product: print cloth. About 1910, the city's largest employer, the American Printing Company (APC), employed 6,000 people and was the largest company printer of cloth in the world. Dozens of other city mills solely produced cloth to be printed at the APC. The city's industry had all its eggs in one, very large basket.

World War I had provided a general increase in demand for textiles, and many of the mills of New England benefited during this time. The post-war economy quickly slowed, however, and production quickly outpaced demand. The Northern mills faced serious competition from

their Southern counterparts due to factors such as lower labor and transportation costs, as well as the South's large investment in new machinery
and other equipment. In 1923, Fall River faced the first wave of mill
closures. Some mills merged and were able to limp along until the late
1920s. By the 1930s and the Great Depression, many more mills were
out of business and the city was bankrupt. A few somehow managed to
survive through World War II and into the 1950s.

The worst fire in Fall River's history occurred on the evening of February 2, 1928. It began when workers were dismantling the recently vacated Pocasset Mill. During the night the fire spread quickly and wiped
out a large portion of downtown. City Hall was spared but was badly
damaged. Today, many of the structures near the corner of North Main
and Bedford Street date from the early 1930s, as they were rebuilt soon
after the fire.

The once mighty American Printing Company finally closed for
good in 1934. In 1937, their huge plant waterfront on Water Street was
acquired by the Firestone Tire & Rubber Company and soon employed
2,600 people. In October 1941, just a few weeks before the attack on
Pearl Harbor, a huge fire broke out in the old 1860s' main building of the
print works. The fire was a major setback to the U.S. war effort, as $15
million in raw rubber (30,000 lbs.) was lost in the inferno.

With the demise of the textile industry, many of the city's mills were
occupied by smaller companies, some in the garment industry, tradition-
ally based in the New York City area but attracted to New England by
the lure of cheap factory space and an eager workforce in need of jobs.
The garment industry survived in the city well into the 1990s but has also
largely become a victim of globalization and foreign competition.

In the 1960s the city's landscape was drastically transformed with
the construction of the Braga Bridge and Interstate 195, which cut directly through the heart of the city. In the wake of the highway building
boom, the city lost some great pieces of its history. The Quequechan
River was filled in and re-routed for much of its length. The historic falls,
which had given the city its name, were diverted into underground culverts. A series of elevated steel viaducts was constructed as to access the
new Braga Bridge. Many historic buildings were demolished, including
the Old City Hall, the 150-year-old Troy Mills, the Second Granite Block

(built after the 1928 fire), as well as other 19th century brick-and-mortar buildings near Old City Hall.

Also during the 1970s, several modern apartment high-rise towers were built throughout the city, many part of the Fall River Housing Authority. In 1978, the city opened the new B.M.C. Durfee High School in the north end, replacing the historic Rock Street masterpiece that had become overcrowded and outdated for use as a high school. The "new" Durfee is one of the largest high schools in Massachusetts.

People of Significance – Fall River

Lizzie Andrew Borden (July 19, 1860 – June 1, 1927) was an American woman who was the main suspect in the August 4, 1892 axe murders of her father and stepmother in Fall River, Massachusetts. Borden was tried and acquitted of the murders.

The case received widespread newspaper coverage throughout the United States. Following her release from jail, where she was held during the trial, Borden chose to remain a resident of Fall River despite facing ostracism from the other residents. The Commonwealth of Massachusetts elected not to charge anyone else with the murder of Andrew and Abby Borden. She spent the remainder of her life in Fall River before dying of pneumonia, aged 66, just days before the death of her sister, Emma.

Borden and her association with the murders has remained a topic in American popular culture mythology into the 21st century, and she has been depicted in various films, theatrical productions, literary works, and folk rhymes, and is still very well known in Fall River and the surrounding area to this day.

Colonel Richard Borden (1795–1874) was an American businessman and civic leader from Fall River, Massachusetts. He co-founded the Fall River Iron Works in 1821, and later built several early cotton mills, as well as the Fall River Line, Fall River Gas Works Company, the Fall River Railroad, banks and other businesses. The Borden family would dominate the economic and civic life of Fall River into the early 20th century.

In 1821, Borden established the Fall River Iron Works, along with Major Bradford Durfee, and several others at the lower part of the Quequechan River. Bradford Durfee was a shipwright, and Richard Borden was the owner of a grist mill. After an uncertain start, in which some early investors pulled out, the Fall River Iron Works was incorporated in 1825, with $200,000 in capital. The Iron Works began producing nails, bar stock, and other items such as bands for casks in the nearby New Bedford whaling industry. They soon gained a reputation for producing nails of high quality, and business flourished.

By 1845, the company was valued at $960,000. In 1827, Borden began regular steamship service to Providence, Rhode Island.

The Iron Works would continue play an important role in the early development of the textile industry in Fall River. Richard Borden later constructed the Metacomet Mill in 1847, which today is the oldest remaining textile mill in the City, located on Agawam Street.

Morton Dean was born on August 22, 1935 in Fall River, the son of Joseph Dubitsky and Celia (Schwartz) Dubitsky. He attended B.M.C. Durfee High School in Fall River. In 1983, the television studio and publications center at the high school was named the Morton Dean Television Studioin his honor and in 2011, Dean was presented the key to the city of Fall River by former mayor William Flanagan.

In 1957, he earned a bachelor's degree in English from Emerson College in Boston. At Emerson, he was captain of the basketball team and president of his fraternity, Alpha Pi Theta. In 1977, he received a Doctor of Law, honorary degree from his alma mater.

George Robert Stephanopoulos was born February 10, 1961, in Fall River and is an American television host, political commentator, and former Democratic advisor. Stephanopoulos currently is chief anchor and political correspondent on ABC News, and a co-anchor with Robin Roberts and Michael Strahan on Good Morning America, and host of This Week, ABC's Sunday morning current events news program.

Before his career as a journalist, Stephanopoulos was an advisor to the Democratic Party. He rose to early prominence as a communications director for Bill Clinton's 1992 presidential campaign and subsequently became White House communications director. He was later senior advisor for policy and strategy, before departing in December 1996.

Eugene Joseph Dionne, Jr. was born in 1952 in Boston but raised in Fall River. Dionne holds an A.B. summa cum laude in Social Studies from Harvard University (1973), where he was elected to Phi Beta Kappa and was affiliated with Adams House. He also earned a DPhil in

Sociology from Balliol College, Oxford (1982), where he was a Rhodes Scholar.

He is an American journalist, political commentator, and long-time op-ed columnist for The Washington Post. He is also a Senior Fellow in Governance Studies at the Brookings Institution, a professor in the Foundations of Democracy and Culture at the McCourt School of Public Policy, Georgetown University, and a commentator for NPR, MSNBC, and PBS.

Margery Eagan (born June 13, 1954), a third-generation Irish-American, was born to Daniel Eagan and Margaret Manning of Fall River and has an older sister, Elizabeth. Eagan was raised Roman Catholic but attended public school. She began writing stories as a child and was encouraged by her English teacher at Durfee High School in Fall River. Eagan attended Smith College her freshman year, then transferred to Stanford University in Palo Alto, California, majoring in American Studies.

She is a talk radio host and a frequent guest on CNN, ABC, and Fox News. For many years she was a columnist for the Boston Herald. Subjects of her commentaries include gender/women's issues, Catholicism, and politics.

Emeril John Lagassé III, born October 15, 1959, in Fall River, is an American celebrity chef, restaurateur, television personality, cookbook author, and National Best Recipe award winner for his 'Turkey and Hot Sausage Chili' recipe in 2003. He is a regional James Beard Award winner, known for his mastery of Creole and Cajun cuisine and his self-developed "New Orleans" style.

Lagasse graduated from the culinary school JWU in 1978 and became Executive Chef at the Dunfey's Hyannis Resort in 1979. He was nominated as Chef of the Year in 1983.

In 1982 Lagasse succeeded Paul Prudhomme as executive chef of Commander's Palace in New Orleans under Richard Brennan, Sr. He led the kitchen there for seven and a half years before leaving to open his own restaurant.

Do You Know – Fall River?

It's the only house in Fall River with a pagoda roof and is constructed of 28 different imported woods. This three-story authentic Japanese-styled house is known as the **"Rising Sun."** Built in 1910, it's on the National Register of Historic Places. It is located at 657 Highland Avenue in Fall River.

Ralph A. Cram, a Boston architect who authored several books on Japanese architecture, designed the house for the Rev. Arthur M. Knapp, pastor of the Unitarian Church. Knapp had been a missionary in Japan and wanted to bring that style of living to his own home.

Kennedy Park (originally known as South Park) is a 57-acre historic park located in the southern part of Fall River. The area of the city where the park is located was until 1862, part of Rhode Island.

The park was originally the farm of John Durfee. The location gained national attention in December 1832, when the pregnant lifeless body of Sarah M. Cornell was found hanging from a stackpole there. Her death was later deemed to be murder. Methodist minister Ephraim K. Avery was accused of the crime, but acquitted after a sensational trial. The verdict outraged many local citizens. Sarah's body was initially buried on the Durfee farm, but moved years later to Oak Grove Cemetery when the park was being built.

Built in 1868, designed by famed 19th century landscape architect Frederick Law Olmsted and Calvert Vaux, the park was originally known as "South Park". The park was renamed in 1963 following the assassination of President John F. Kennedy.

The city of Fall River was originally home to the **Wampanoag Native American tribe,** but this group was displaced relatively rapidly in the 1600s with the establishment of colonies in modern day Massachusetts, Rhode Island, and Connecticut.

In 1936, the **Federal One Division of the Works Progress** Administration commissioned artist **John Mann** to create a mural or series of murals depicting the history of Fall River.

The Federal One project was intended to provide work for artists, writers, playwrights, and musicians during the Great Depression to ensure that our nation's cultural heritage did not diminish due to the economic crisis. John Mann studied the history of the city and after four months of intense research began to paint a chronological history of Fall River that spanned from the Native American tribes to the Cotton Industry era. Through the facilities of the Public Library and the Fall River Historical Society and with the cooperation of many of Fall River's oldest families, he was able to obtain much information concerning early Fall River history. Mann choose the subjects of the paintings at his own discretion and, judging from the finished products he succeeded in making fascinating choices. The murals were painted in the auditorium of the B.M.C Durfee High School Technical Building, later the Matthew J. Kuss Middle School and currently the Resiliency Preparatory School.

There are three sets of murals, each depicting a different era in Fall River's history. The first mural series contains six panels about Native American history. The second mural recreates Fall River's history from the Revolutionary War to the Civil War. The last mural centers on the history of Fall River in the cotton mill era.

When **the Braga Bridge** was built, the Quequechan River was filled in and re-routed for much of its length. The historic falls, which had given the city its name, were diverted into underground culverts. The bridge was named after Charles M. Braga, a Fall River native of Portuguese American descent who was killed in the attack on Pearl Harbor.

Santo Christo Parish is known as the Mother Church of the Portuguese Parishes in the Fall River Diocese. The Church was established in 1892 to serve the local Portuguese community that immigrated predominately from the São Miguel Island of Azores.

The seat of **the Roman Catholic Diocese** of Fall River, located at St. Mary's Cathedral on Second Street, formed in the 1850s by Irish immigrants.

With Five National Historic Landmark US Naval ships and other craft, **Battleship Cove** is America's Fleet Museum. The attractions include what it was like to serve on board a Navy warship in WWII and the Vietnam War era, dive into a submarine and explore a high-speed missile corvette that was built by the Soviet Union.

BMC Durfee High School - the building was built as a donation from Mrs. Mary B. Young to the people of the city of Fall River, in memory of her son Bradford Matthew Chaloner Durfee, who had died at a young age in 1872, leaving a sizable inheritance.

The mansion that houses the **Fall River Historical Society** dates to 1843. It was built on a two-acre piece of land on Columbia Street – a wedding gift from Andrew Robeson to his son and daughter-in-law. In the 1850s, it became a stop on the Underground Railroad where slaves were invited through a false bookcase that still exists and hidden in the wine cellar. The house was moved to 451 Rock Street in 1869 and founded as the Fall River Historical Society in 1921. Besides historic furniture and household items from Fall River families, it houses the largest-known collection of Lizzie Borden memorabilia.

The **current city hall** sits on a site over Rte. 195 which is over the site of the former City Hall that burned down during the great fire of 1928.

The **Children's Museum of Fall River** is made up of a number of theme rooms. The dinosaur pit, the Lego room, the water room, etc. are bright and airy with imaginative set-ups and lots to keep kids busy. It is located in the former Bristol County Superior Court building.

The well that serviced the **Lafayette–Durfee House** located at 94 Cherry Street in Fall River, Massachusetts is still visible behind the former Bristol County Courthouse that currently sits on the site. The house was originally owned by Judge Thomas Durfee. While the exact date of its construction is not known, it is estimated to have been built before 1750.

The **influenza epidemic** came to Fall River in the fall of 1918. Between September 16 and the end of 1918, 11,707 cases of influenza were reported to the Fall River Board of Health. Of these cases, 719 died. For the period when the disease was considered epidemic – September 16 to October 31 – Fall River experienced 10,624 cases and 629 deaths.

Copicut Woods is a 1.6 mile moderately trafficked loop trail located in Fall River/Freetown State Forest, that features a great forest setting and is good for all skill levels. The trail offers a number of activity options and is accessible year-round. Dogs are also able to use this trail but must be kept on leash. There are great trails, lots of variety, stone walls, cobbles and roots, and open bridges. Great for dogs. Wetland too.

Quequechan River Rail Trail was started in 2015 and completed in 2017. It travels along the northern shore of scenic South Watuppa Pond. The project created a ten-foot-wide paved surface with three-foot grass shoulders that runs over a former railroad bed and five boardwalks to connect with Britland Park and Rodman Street. This multi-use path in the heart of Fall River is dedicated to Alfred J. Lima. It was his inspiration and design that was the catalyst for this path.

Did you know the following were Major League Baseball players that graduated from B.M.C. Durfee High School?

Mark Bomback - Former MLB player (Milwaukee Brewers, New York Mets, Toronto Blue Jays)

Tom Gastall - Former MLB player (Baltimore Orioles)

Russ Gibson - Former MLB player (Boston Red Sox, San Francisco Giants)

Brandon Gomes - Former MLB player (Tampa Bay Rays)

Andrew Sousa - Former MLS Player (New England Revolution)

Luke Urban - Former MLB player (Boston Braves).

All About Marion

Marion is a town in Plymouth County, Massachusetts. The population was 4,907 at the 2010 census.

Marion was first settled in 1679 as "Sippican," a district of Rochester, Massachusetts. The name, which also lends itself to the river that passes through the north of town and the harbor at the heart of town, was the Wampanoag named for the local tribe. The town was mostly known for its many local sea captains and sailors whose homes were in town, although there were some small shipbuilding operations on the harbor. By the late 1840s, however, tensions between the village of Mattapoisett and the town led to a battle that sought to redraw the town lines and effectively take over Sippican Village. The stress caused the villagers to form a committee, which went to Boston to petition for incorporation. Thus, with the help of a powerful local ally, the town was incorporated on May 14, 1852, and renamed Marion in honor of Revolutionary War hero Francis Marion. Mattapoisett was incorporated in 1857.

Since that time, Marion's economy has mostly relied on the waters of Buzzards Bay, both for boating, fishing and for the summer tourism industry. Recreational sailing is a significant seasonal activity for residents and visitors.

Marion is located on Buzzards Bay, and its geography is shaped by the water. Much of the town is separated into two halves by Sippican Harbor, with Converse Point to the west and Sippican Neck to the east. Marion has several parks and piers, beaches, Marion is a typical old New England town with a small quaint village with many traditional Cape Cod-style homes. The village includes The Marion General Store that dates back to the 1800s.

It is the home of the noted Marion Indoor Tennis Club as well as the Beverly Yacht Club, and The Kittansett Golf Club.

People of Significance – Marion

Benjamin Spooner Briggs (April 24, 1835 – likely November 1872) was an experienced seaman and master mariner. He was the Captain of the merchant ship Mary Celeste, which was discovered unmanned and drifting in the Atlantic Ocean midway between the Azores and the coast of Portugal on December 4, 1872. The lifeboat was missing, yet the Mary Celeste herself was still under sail. Benjamin Briggs, his wife Sarah, and their two-year-old daughter Sophia Matilda were never found and are presumed lost, along with the crew of Mary Celeste.

Elizabeth Taber (1791-1888) was born in Marion, attended the Sippican Seminary, which was the equivalent to a modern high school and the only center of learning beyond grammar school in Marion in the 19th century. Elizabeth ultimately became a teacher and taught in Marion before marrying clockmaker Stephen Taber and settling in New Bedford.

Following her husband's death, Elizabeth returned to Marion as a wealthy widow with a mission to revive the town of Marion. She established the Elizabeth Taber Library and the Natural History Museum; she built what is now known as the Music Hall, and she contributed a significant sum to build the Marion Town Hall.

Most of all, however, Elizabeth Taber sought to devote her life to education. In 1876, at the age of 85, she established Tabor Academy.

Dominic Paul DiMaggio (February 12, 1917 – May 8, 2009), nicknamed "The Little Professor," was an American Major League Baseball center fielder. He played his entire 11-year baseball career for the Boston Red Sox (1940–1953). DiMaggio was the youngest of three brothers who became major league center fielders, the others being Joe and Vince.

In 1959, DiMaggio joined forces with nine other New Englanders, led by Billy Sullivan, to found and capitalize a Boston American football team that debuted in 1960 as the AFL's Boston Patriots.

Famous Summer Residents

Franklin Delano Roosevelt (January 30, 1882 – April 12, 1945), often referred to by his initials FDR, was an American politician who served as the 32nd president of the United States from 1933 until he died in 1945. A member of the Democratic Party, he won a record four presidential elections and became a central figure in world events during the first half of the 20th century. Roosevelt directed the federal government during most of the Great Depression, implementing his New Deal domestic agenda in response to the worst economic crisis in U.S. history. As a dominant leader of his party, he built the New Deal Coalition, which realigned American politics into the Two Party System and defined modern liberalism in the United States throughout the middle third of the 20th century. His third and fourth terms were dominated by World War II, which ended shortly after he died in office.

Rear Admiral Richard Evelyn Byrd Jr. (October 25, 1888 – March 11, 1957) was an American naval officer and explorer. He was a recipient of the Medal of Honor, the highest honor for valor given by the United States, and was a pioneering American aviator, polar explorer, and organizer of polar logistics. Aircraft flights in which he served as a navigator and expedition leader crossed the Atlantic Ocean, a segment of the Arctic Ocean, and a part of the Antarctic Plateau. Byrd claimed that his expeditions had been the first to reach both the North Pole and the South Pole by air. His claim to have reached the North Pole is disputed. He is also known for discovering Mount Sidley, the largest dormant volcano in Antarctica, in 1934.

Henry James OM (April 15, 1843 – February 28, 1916) was an American author who became a British subject in the last year. He is regarded as a key transitional figure between literary realism and literary modernism and is considered by many to be among the greatest novelists in the English language. He was Henry James Sr. and the brother of renowned philosopher and psychologist William James and diarist Alice James.

Do You Know – Marion?

The town of Marion has a total area of 26 square miles, and 12.1 square miles of that area is covered by water.

The **Beverly Yacht Club** was founded in 1872 in Beverly, Massachusetts. Its purpose was to provide a place where yachts under 30 feet in length at the waterline could participate in races. Its founding dates back to a dinner in Boston attended by Edward and Walter Burgess. Walter Burgess was a famous yacht designer. Its first races were held in the summer of 1872 in Beverly. The Club expanded to Wings Neck in 1895, where it leased a clubhouse. As its membership increased in Wings Neck, it moved to Marion in 1913.

The **Stone Estate** at Great Hill, owned by the Stone family, is on a peninsula that juts out into Buzzards Bay and consists of 312 acres of rolling woods, meadows, and lawns. The prominent feature of this property is a distinctive glacial hill that reaches 127 feet above sea level and gives the estate its name. It is the highest land in Marion and has approximately two-and-one-half miles of waterfront. The Hill Family owns the property with a large mansion and 10 Hill family homes on the property.

Great Hill is also the home of the Great Hill Dairy, Inc., that has been known for its outstanding herd of Guernsey cows and its prize-winning Acacia and Orchid collections. Great Hill now produces an award-winning unique tasting blue cheese made in its turn-of-the-century barn known as Great Hill Blue, a gourmet non-homogenized raw milk Blue Cheese.

Marion is home to one of the largest **sailing fleets** in Massachusetts, showing a forest of masts in the inner harbor during the summer months. Directly adjacent to the Harbormaster is a small shellfish area that is stocked by the town. There is a public beach at the end of Front St. It is groomed and has a lifeguard station.

The **Marion Natural History Society** defines Natural History as including zoology, botany, mineralogy, geology, and all other issues which pertain to these subjects, including the past and present lifestyles of man and his treatment of his environment. The mission of the Marion Natural History Museum is to promote public interest in and knowledge of natural history to increase our visitors' awareness of man's relationship within his environment. The Museum is located in the Town Library at 8 Spring Street, Marion.

Marion is the home of the nationally recognized construction company, **South Coast Improvement**. The founder, Tom Quinlan, is assisted by his brother, former ORR football coach Henry Quinlan and his sister Sarah Murphy and a large staff. They have built buildings as far away as Seattle, WA, and Fort Lauderdale, FL. South Coast has a branch office in Reading, PA. Besides its work in the healthcare field, it has extensive experience in the education world as it has completed projects at Boston College, Boston University, Harvard University, Massachusetts Institute of Technology and Northeastern University.

Bird Island is a tiny island in Buzzards Bay at the mouth of Sippican Harbor, less than a mile off the mainland coast of the town of Marion, Massachusetts. The only landmarks on Bird Island are a flagpole and a historic 36-foot-high lighthouse. Bird Island Light was formerly manned but now runs automatically. The Great New England Hurricane caused widespread destruction all along the south coast of New England. High tide in the evening of September 21, 1938, was 14 feet above normal. The great storm swept away every building on Bird Island except the lighthouse tower.

Bird Island and Nix's Mate Island in Boston Harbor were used for gibbeting pirates and sailors executed for crimes in Massachusetts. Their bodies were left hanging as a warning to sailors coming into the harbor and approaching Boston.

The Marion General Store has served the community for 44 years. If you count the building's previous incarnations as a Congregational Church Meeting House and other retail options, it's been around for 224 years. It has recently been refurbished and now has a few tables for eating inside.

The 2020 edition of the **Buzzards Bay Musicfest** was canceled but plans are being made for the 2021 edition according to Co- Founder Trudy Kingery and Honorary Chairperson of the board along with Charles Stegeman – Artistic Director. It will be the 24th year for the Musicfest in pursuing its mission of providing free concerts for the cultural enrichment of the residents of the area. By design, all concerts are free. It was the mission of the Musicfest's founding members to provide an extraordinary opportunity for cultural enrichment to the public –without cost. It is staged at Tabor Academy's Fireman Center.

In its first year the Musicfest housed all of the musicians in the dorms of Tabor Academy. Any worries that some of the internationally and nationally known musicians would complain was quickly dissipated as the musicians were all in on the basic concept of the Musicfest, providing free concerts.

The Marion Sports Shop is renowned more for the quality of its selection of clothing for men and women than it is for sporting equipment. When you want to buy good quality and stylist clothing this is your first stop and if it is not in stock the owner, Frank Fletcher, will get it for you.

Marion is also home to some of the finest yacht yards around, with **Burr Brothers** at the very head of the harbor offering docking, rental moorings and a full service marina. Burr Brothers has a great aerial shot of the harbor on their website.

The **Marion to Bermuda Cruising Yacht Rac**e is a biennial yacht race held in odd-numbered years, from Marion to the island of Bermuda, a distance of 645 nautical miles. The race defines itself as a "Corinthian" event, that is, one where the owners of the boats are part of the sailing crew and the crew is not paid to take part in the event.

The original **Tabor Academy** buildings were deeded to the town (now the Elizabeth Taber Library and Marion Town Hall) and were traded for the current waterfront location in order to allow the academy to expand and grow. The school acquired the surrounding cottages and plots of land in order to secure the academy's future expansion.

All About Mattapoisett

Mattapoisett is a town in Plymouth County, Massachusetts. The population was 6,045 at the 2010 census.

The Mattapoisett area was originally purchased by Governor William Brenton from the Wampanoag chief Metacomet, also referred to as King Philip, in 1664. Brenton left it to his son Ebenezer, who sold it. The town of Mattapoisett was settled in 1750 and officially incorporated in 1857. Originally a part of Rochester, the area had most likely been visited by European traders and sailors. There is also evidence of prior Wampanoag Indian settlements, including burial grounds, throughout the town. In fact, the word Mattapoisett is Wampanoag for "a place of resting".

Early industry included logging and farming, but Mattapoisett became best known for its role in the history of whaling. Some 400 ships were built in the town's shipyards from 1740 until the 1870s, including the Acushnet, the ship that Moby-Dick author Herman Melville sailed on and later deserted. The town supplied many of the whalers used on the East Coast in the first half of the nineteenth century. The last one, the Wanderer, was built in 1878, shortly after the discovery of oil in Pennsylvania, which led to the demise of commercial whaling in the United States.

With the decline of whaling and associated shipbuilding, Mattapoisett transitioned into a popular summer vacation spot for prominent New York and Boston residents, including Oliver Wendell Holmes, Jr. Today, the town is largely a suburban community, with most residents commuting to jobs in greater New Bedford, Providence or Boston, or operating businesses targeting summer tourism.

People of Significance – Mattapoisett

Francis Davis Millet (November 3, 1848 – April 15, 1912) was an American academic classical painter, sculptor, and writer who died in the sinking of the RMS Titanic on April 15, 1912. Francis Davis Millet was born in Mattapoisett, Massachusetts. Most sources give his date of birth as November 3, 1846, but a diary which he kept during his military service stated that November 3, 1864 was his 16th birthday, indicating birth in 1848. At age fifteen, Millet entered the Massachusetts regiment, first as a drummer boy and then a surgical assistant helping his father, a surgeon in the American Civil War.

He repeatedly pointed to his experience working for his father as giving him an appreciation for the vivid blood red that he frequently used in his early paintings. He graduated from Harvard with a Master of Arts degree. He worked as a reporter and editor for the Boston Courier and then as a correspondent for the Advertiser at the Philadelphia Centennial Exposition.

Elizabeth Drew Barstow was born May 6, 1823, in the small coastal town of Mattapoisett, Massachusetts. She received a thorough education in various boarding-schools and in her school-days showed her bent towards poetry and literature in general. She studied at Wheaton Seminary, Norton, Massachusetts.

Soon after her marriage to Richard Henry Stoddard, the author, she began to publish poems in all the leading magazines, and thereafter, she was a frequent contributor. Her verses were of a high order; she wrote for intellectual readers only. She never collected the numerous poems she published in the periodicals, although there were enough of them to fill a large volume. In addition to her poetical productions, she published three novels: *The Morgesons* (New York City, 1862); *Two Men* (1865), and *Temple House* (1867). Those books did not find a large sale when first published, but a second edition, published in 1888, found a wider circle of readers. They were pictures of New England scenes and characters. In 1874, she published *Lolly Dinks's Doings*, a juvenile story.

52

Samuel Atkinson Waterston, born November 15, 1940), is an American actor, producer, and director. Waterston is known for his work in theater, television and film. Waterston, having studied at the Sorbonne in Paris and the American Actors Workshop, started his career in theater on the New York stage, appearing in multiple revivals of Shakespeare. In 1977, he starred in an off-Broadway production of Measure for Measure as Duke Vincentio alongside Meryl Streep and John Cazale at the Delacorte Theatre.

Sam Waterston, the third of four siblings (Roberta, George, and Ellen), was born in Cambridge, Massachusetts. His mother, Alice Tucker (née Atkinson), a landscape painter, was of English ancestry, and a descendant of Mayflower passengers. His father, George Chychele Waterston, was an emigrant from Leith, Scotland, and a semanticist and language teacher. He now lives in Mattapoisett.

Milton Silveira was born in Mattapoisett, Massachusetts, in 1929. His parents, Antonne and Carolinda Silveira, were immigrants from the Azores. His love of aeronautics began at age 16, when he acquired his pilot's license. Silveira attended Fairhaven High School, and gained a BSc in mechanical engineering from the University of Vermont, where he was president of the flying club.

In June 1951, Silveira joined NASA's predecessor, the National Advisory Committee for Aeronautics (NACA), in Langley, Virginia. In September 1951, he was called to duty as an army aviator by the United States Army and later served as the Chief Engineering and Maintenance Officer of the U.S. 8th Army in Korea. In 1955, he returned to NACA. He continued his education simultaneously – in 1960, he received an MSc in aeronautical engineering from the University of Virginia, and he conducted post-graduate work at Virginia Tech and the University of Houston between 1960 and 1968.

In 1983, after nearly a decade of mid-level involvement with the Space Shuttle program, Silveira became NASA's Chief Engineer. In the aftermath of the Space Shuttle Challenger disaster in January 1986.

Do You Know – Mattapoisett?

Mattapoisett is a word from the **Indian language**, and said to signify rest.

Indians living a few miles back from the seaboard used frequently to come down to the shore at this place for the purpose of obtaining fish and clams, and at an adjoining spring stopped to rest, and hence the name that they gave that locality, the river, and some of the surrounding country.

Ned's Point Beach is located straight ahead when driving into the park. Here you can go swimming, boating, and enjoy other beach activities. There are bathrooms conveniently located on the grounds as well as a picnic dining area. Although a town-owned beach, most days you'll be the only person on it! See Ned's Point Lighthouse across the beautiful harbor; go at low tide and walk across to Shining Tides Beach – a great spot for quohogging.

The Mattapoisett Historical Society is housed in an 1821 Meeting House with an attached replica of a 200-year-old carriage house. The ancient pews, graceful galleries, and post and beam construction in the carriage house carry one back to when life revolved around work, church, town meeting and the waterfront.

The Center School, donated by Mr. Rogers, has served Mattapoisett well, but it was not the end of Rogers' beneficence to the town. When Fairhaven High School was finished in 1906, Mr. Rogers directed that Mattapoisett students were to use its superior facilities as long as population levels made accommodation feasible. Young people of Mattapoisett attended Fairhaven High School until June, 1961 when crowded classrooms and strained facilities broke off a long and distinguished relationship. Mary Jean Schmidt, leader of a student panel discussion at the 1961 graduation said:

"For fifty-five years' students from Fairhaven and Mattapoisett have shared good days together at **Fairhaven High School.**

Contributions that Mattapoisett students have made to the high school are innumerable and ties formed between the students from the two towns have been deep and lasting. Indeed, it has not been until impending separation has threatened that we have fully realized the value of this school union. Now, with the building of the **Old Rochester Regional High School**, Mattapoisett students will no longer accompany us to classes, and a pleasant and profitable relationship of more than half a century will be terminated."

At the annual **town meeting** in Mattapoisett in 1907 — a resolution acknowledged Mr. Rogers' further kindness to the town. It stated:

"Resolved that this town now assembled in annual meeting record its appreciation and express its thanks to Mr. Henry H. Rogers for his generous thoughtfulness in that having furnished a magnificently equipped High School to the town of Fairhaven, he has directed that its privileges and benefits be now made free for such time as they can be accommodated — to the pupils of Mattapoisett, and thereby has made a contribution to education in this community which will continue as a blessing to its children for some years to come."

A **new elevated bike path** is being built in 2020 in Mattapoisett.

The **elevated bike path** that is being built over wetlands and estuaries in Mattapoisett is going to have a breathtaking view as it passes from the Mattapoisett River to the Reservation Golf Course. And that bike path is ahead of schedule and will someday extend all the way through town. The pilings of the elevated bike path that have been erected over wetlands and estuaries in Mattapoisett are part of a boardwalk that will go from the Mattapoisett River Bridge to property at the Reservation Golf Course, totaling 600 linear feet, 14-feet wide. Here, the project is using donated land the nearby YMCA Camp Massasoit. Also, an 1800-foot board walk and bridge is being built across the railroad right of way at the western breech of Eel Pond, which will result in an 800 foot, eight-foot wide boardwalk.

Karsten Rathlev has been appointed the head of Tennis at the Bay Club. He is also the owner of the Marion Indoor Tennis Club. He was the coach of the UMass Dartmouth men's tennis team until it was disbanded this year because of budget cuts.

The **Mattapoisett Community Sailing Association, Inc. (MattSail)** was incorporated in 2007 to provide a safe and affordable sailing education program for the residents of Mattapoisett, Marion & Rochester. The initial and signature program is the William E. Mee Youth Sailing Program which consists of three two-week sessions for students ages 6 to 13.

MattSail also sponsors the coed High School Sailing Team at Old Rochester Regional High School. The goal is to develop and grow a competitive team.

There is also an Adult Sailing Instructional Program to teach basic sailing nomenclature and safety rules to adult beginner sailors or for adult sailors who need to build confidence in their sailing ability.

The **Mattapoisett Historical Society** has launched a new project entitled **"These Old Homes."** The Society is collecting fun facts and fables about homes that are more than 50 years old. Every month a different house will be featured on the Mattapoisett Historical Society website.

All About New Bedford

New Bedford is a city in Bristol County, Massachusetts. As of the 2010 census, the city had a total population of 95,072, making it the sixth-largest city in Massachusetts. New Bedford is nicknamed "The Whaling City" because it was one of the world's most important whaling ports in the nineteenth century, along with Nantucket, Massachusetts, and New London, Connecticut. New Bedford and Fall River are the two largest cities in the South Coast region of Massachusetts. The New Bedford is known for its fishing fleet and accompanying seafood industry and its high concentration of Portuguese Americans.

Before the 17th century, the Wampanoag Native Americans, who had settlements throughout southeastern Massachusetts and Rhode Island, including Martha's Vineyard and Nantucket, were the only inhabitants of the lands Acushnet River. While exploring New England, Bartholomew Gosnold landed on Cuttyhunk Island on May 15, 1602. From there, he explored Cape Cod and the neighboring areas, including the site of present-day New Bedford. However, rather than settle the area, he returned to England at the request of his crew.

A group of English Quakers from the Plymouth Colony—who as pacifists held ideological differences with the Puritans on the question of taxes to fund a military—separated and established the first European settlement on the South Coast in 1652. They purchased Old Dartmouth—a region that is now Dartmouth, Acushnet, New Bedford, Fairhaven, and Westport—from Chief Massasoit of the native Wampanoag to start a new society.

A section of Old Dartmouth near the west bank of the Acushnet River, originally called Bedford Village, was officially incorporated as the town of New Bedford on February 23, 1787, after the American Revolutionary War. The name was suggested by the Russell family, who were prominent citizens of the community. The Dukes of Bedford, a leading English aristocratic house, also bore the surname Russell. (Bedford, Massachusetts had been incorporated in 1729; hence "New" Bedford.).

The American Revolutionary War completely paralyzed the whaling industry. British forces blockaded American ports and captured or destroyed American commercial ships; they even marched down King's Street in New Bedford (defiantly renamed Union Street after the Revolution) and set businesses on fire.

Nantucket was even more exposed, and the physical destruction, frozen economy, and import taxes imposed after the War obliterated previous fortunes. New Bedford also had a deeper harbor and was located on the mainland. As a result, New Bedford supplanted Nantucket as the nation's preeminent whaling port, and so began the Golden Age of Whaling.

After the War of 1812's embargo was lifted, New Bedford started amassing some colossal, sturdy, square-rigged whaling ships, many of them built at the shipyard of Mattapoisett. The invention of on-board try-works, a system of massive iron pots over a brick furnace, allowed the whalers to render high-quality oil from the blubber. This allowed the whaling ships to go out to sea for as long as four years, processing their catch while at sea. Ships from New Bedford came back to port with barrels of oil, spermaceti, and occasionally ambergris.

Whaling dominated New Bedford's economy for much of the century, and many families of the city were involved with it as crew and officers of ships. The Quakers remained prominent and influential in New Bedford throughout the whaling era. They brought religious values into their business models, promoting stability and prosperity, investing in infrastructure projects such as rail, and employing without discrimination. They established solid social and economic relationships with Boston, New York, and Philadelphia, integrating New Bedford into the northeastern urban economy.

Ten thousand men worked in the whaling industry. During this period, New Bedford's population increased from approximately 4,000 in 1820 to about 24,000 in 1860. At the height of the whaling industry in 1857, the harbor hosted 329 vessels worth over $12 million, and New Bedford became the wealthiest city per capita in the world.

On March 18, 1847, the town of New Bedford officially became a city; Abraham Hathaway Howland was elected its first mayor.

The Quakers of New Bedford applied their principles of egalitarianism and community-building in their businesses. On the boats, at the docks, at the factories, or in the shops—British, Wampanoag, Cape Verdean, Azorean, Irish, and West African hands found work in New Bedford. New Bedford also became one of the first fermentation centers of abolitionism in North America and an important stop on the Underground Railroad.

The textile mills redefined wealth in New Bedford and gave birth to prosperity greater than that of the whaling industry. New Bedford, funded by industrial fortunes, developed a thriving art scene. The Mount Washington Glass Company (which later became Pairpoint) crafted works of glass and silver for the newly affluent class, and examples of these works can be seen today on the second floor of the New Bedford Whaling Museum.

Despite the historical decline of fishing and whaling in New England, New Bedford continues to be a leading fishing port. In 2019, New Bedford was the highest-valued port in the nation, a title it has held for seventeen straight years. $327 million worth of seafood crossed its docks, making it more valuable than even the most productive Alaskan fishing ports. While volume is below other major ports, New Bedford retains its top position due mainly to its scallop fishing.

Fishing and manufacturing continue to be two of the largest businesses in the area, and healthcare has become a significant employer. The three largest single employers based in New Bedford are Southcoast Hospitals Group, one of the top ten employers in Massachusetts (healthcare), Titleist (golf clubs, balls, apparel, manufacturing), and Riverside Manufacturing (apparel manufacturing).

People of Significance – New Bedford

Robert's Rules of Order was written in New Bedford by **Henry M. Roberts**. He wrote, in 1876, the manual in response to his poor performance in leading a church meeting that erupted into open conflict because of concerns about local defense at the First Baptist Church, 149 William Street in New Bedford, Massachusetts. He resolved that he would learn about parliamentary procedures before attending another meeting. He was an American soldier and engineer and was stationed in New Bedford when he wrote the Rules of Order.

New Bedford born **Henrietta Howland "Hetty" Green: the "Witch of Wall Street,"** was the wealthiest woman in the world in the late 1800s and early 1900s in the era known as the Gilded Age. The sole heiress of the wealthiest whaling dynasty in the richest city in America, Hetty Howland Robinson Green, multiplied several million dollars into what today would be several billion dollars through her investment strategies on Wall Street. Her sole business was investing in real estate, stocks, and bonds. She was an innovator in the field of value investing.

James Arnold came to New Bedford and married into one of the founding whaling industry families. Whaling merchant, whose estate is now known as the Wamsutta Club in New Bedford. In 1821 he erected a Federal Style brick mansion along with extensive gardens. He opened the private gardens to the public, at the time an unusual and highly regard act. The mansion later became the Wamsutta Mansion. He died in 1868 and bequeathed $100,000 to support agricultural and horticulture programs. His trustees decided to give the money to Harvard College, which set up the Arnold Arboretum in Boston.

In 1840 **Herman Melville** went to New Bedford, where he signed up for a whaling voyage aboard a new ship, the Acushnet. Built-in 1840, the ship measured some 104 feet in length, almost 28 feet in breadth, and nearly 14 feet in depth. Melville signed a contract on Christmas Day with the ship's agent as a "green hand" for 1/175th of whatever profits the voyage would yield. On January 3, 1841, the Acushnet set sail. In 1842

Melville jumped ship when the ship was at the Marquesas Islands. His book, *Moby Dick,* based on his experiences on the Acushnet, was published in 1852. The premier for the movie *Moby Dick* was held in New Bedford on June 27, 1956, with Gregory Peck in attendance.

Frederick Douglas, as Fred Bailey boarded a train in Baltimore in 1838, escaped north to freedom dressed in a sailor's uniform stitched by his fiancée, a free woman, Anna Murray. His escape route on the underground railroad would take him to New York, Newport, Rhode Island, and finally to New Bedford, MA, where he received the help of Nathan and Polly Johnson, well known African American abolitionists. It is in New Bedford that Frederick Douglass and his bride, Anna began their life together and raised their young family.

By the 1960s, Berkshire Hathaway, founded in 1888 by Horatio Hathaway, had declined to seven plants and 6,000 employees but still annually produced one-quarter of a billion yards of material that sold for more than $60 million. The assets, and a sizable amount of cash on the balance sheet, caught the eye of Warren Buffett, an up-and-coming but little-known investor from Omaha, Nebraska. Through his Buffett Partnership Limited investment firm Buffett started buying stock in Berkshire at $7.60 per share. He eventually paid an average of $14.86 cents a share or a total of $14 million and took control of the company on May 10, 1965.

Clifford Warren Ashley: Author, sailor, and artist, most famous for "The Ashley Book of Knots," an encyclopedic reference manual, copiously illustrated, on the tying of thousands of knots. He invented Ashley's stopper knot.

Patrick Cunningham was an Irish immigrant who lived in New Bedford. He was an inventor known for building a torpedo, which he later fired down a street in the city during a political rally. The torpedo collided with a building before he exploded and caused severe damage to the building.

Bishop "Sweet Daddy" Grace, a native of Brava, Cape Verde, was a New Bedford resident who founded the United House of Prayer for All People, one of the largest African-American sects in America. Grace was quoted as saying, "I do these things in Jesus' name." He died with an estate of $25 million and is buried in New Bedford.

Do You Know – New Bedford?

The world's largest model whaling ship, the **Lagoda**, is a half-scale model built-in 1915-16. It is one of many treasures in the Whaling Museum.

Youghal Ireland was chosen to portray the 1860s New Bedford in the 1956 film *Moby Dick*. In 2011 the mayor of Youghal visited to give a lecture on the making of the movie and the positive effect that it had on their community. Youghal also has an annual Moby Dick Festival.

There is a New Bedford Museum in **Mindelo Cape Verde**, a major port and the departure city for many Cape Verdeans who come to New Bedford.

Funchal is the capital of Madeira and a Sister City to New Bedford. The connection between Madeira and New Bedford started in the 1870s when Madeirans began to immigrate to New Bedford in search of opportunities in new emerging industries.

There is a **Massachusetts Whale Trail**. It is a one-of-a-kind collection of sites, stories, and adventures. The Massachusetts Whale Trail links nearly 40 museums, attractions, whale watching excursions, historic sites, and tours dedicated to our unique connection with these beloved creatures of the deep.

The **New Bedford Symphony Orchestra** welcomes newcomers with a guide; but if you like music, any kind of music, there's a really good chance that you'll like classical music, too. The NBSO is not your great-great-grandfather's symphony orchestra!"

This welcoming statement is followed by much more information on its website.

The **New Bedford Festival Theatre** was founded in 1990 by Armand Marchand and has presented 26 summers of fully mounted musical productions that have entertained over nearly 300,000 theatre-goers.

The **William Rotch Jr. House**, now the Rotch–Jones–Duff House and Garden Museum, is a National Historic Landmark at 396 County Street in New Bedford. The three families whose names are attached to it were closely tied to the city's nineteenth-century dominance of the whaling industry. Because of this, the house is part of the New Bedford Whaling National Historical Park.

The **New Bedford Fire Museum** is housed in a red-brick building, formerly Fire Station No. 4, which opened in 1867. The museum has a collection of old firefighting equipment and some old fire engines. Old city fire records dating to 1890 are available for research and review. Retired and active city firefighters act as docents.

The **New Bedford Museum of Glass** has a comprehensive collection of glass ranging from ancient Mediterranean unguent bottles to designs by contemporary artists such as Dale Chihuly.

New Bedford has **nine historic districts** on the National Register of Historic Places. Locals refer to New Bedford and Fall River as New Beige and The Rivah, respectively.

Fort Tabor was initially built as a lighthouse during the thriving whaling days of the 1800s. Here you can find panoramic views of the water and surrounding peninsulas.

The **New Bedford Whaling Museum** is home to a massive whale skeleton oozing whale oil for over 15 years. It's one of only four blue whale skeletons on display globally, and the museum has been collecting the drippings into a small beaker. Whale oil will occasionally splat onto the floor or guests.

The city is home to **three radio stations**: FM stations WJFD-FM/97.3 (Portuguese-language) and WNBH-FM/101.3, and WNBH-AM/1340. All three have served the residents of New Bedford for many decades.

The New Bedford Whaling Museum hosts an annual marathon reading of the whaling classic, *Moby Dick*.

The first **Wamsutta mill** was a granite block mill, which opened in 1848. It was of New Bedford's few granite mills. Later structures were solidly constructed of brick. Eventually, there were eight mills that made up the Wamsutta complex, with 236,000 spindles and 7,300 looms. It had the reputation of producing very fine cotton sheeting.

About the **year 1920**, there were in New Bedford, 28 cotton establishments, operating 70 mills, having 3,594,138 spindles, 5,679 looms and employing 41,380 operatives.

Today, many more residents are descendants of mill workers and not from people who worked in the whaling industry.

In 1858 **oil was discovered** in Pennsylvania, which was the beginning of the end of the whaling industry in New Bedford. Investors whose wealth came from whaling now turned to building textile mills in New Bedford.

During **New Bedford's textile heyday**, the mills employed more than 41,000 workers. Ten-hour days were the norm for full-time workers; eight hours for part-timers. The work was monotonous and grinding. But the millworkers showed up day after day because if they didn't, there were many others eager to take their jobs.

In 1928 the **mill workers struck**. The strike was settled with the workers receiving a 5% wage cut. The mill owners responded by increasing the speed of the looms, so the weavers had more looms to tend.

Most of the **mills closed** not because they moved south but because of the depression.

Fort Rodman, as built-in 1857, had emplacements for 72 cannon in three tiers; a fourth tier was originally planned, but this was removed from the design to allow more timely completion. Construction was halted in 1871, and the fort as planned was never completed.

The **Clarks Point Light** stands on the parapet of Fort Rodman. Originally established as a freestanding tower, it was moved to the fort in 1869 because its walls obscured the beacon from some angles. It was deactivated in 1898 but was relit in 2001 by the city as a private aid to navigation.

In 1898 the entire military property **was named in honor of Lt. Col. William Rodman** of New Bedford, who was killed in the Civil War. Many people today refer to it as Ft. Taber.

During the **war in Sept. 1778**, roughly 4,000 British troops attacked four villages on the Acushnet River. Ships, businesses, and homes in New Bedford, Acushnet, and Fairhaven were destroyed. The fort at Nolscot Point — now Fort Phoenix — was also demolished. It took years for the local waterfront industries to recover from the raid.

From the whalers, fishermen, and mill workers who settled here in the 19th and early 20th centuries to the Azoreans who began arriving in large numbers in the 1960s, Portuguese people have played a vital role in the region's immigration story.

Now a new initiative at the University of Massachusetts Lowell will be providing a window into that history and into the unique cultural traditions **that Portuguese-Americans** have brought to such communities as Lowell, Lawrence, Gloucester, and Hudson.

The **Greater Boston Portuguese-American Digital Archive**, which the center is developing in collaboration with the UMass Lowell Libraries Center for Lowell History, will allow free access to the public, according to Frank Sousa, founding director of the six-year-old Saab Center.

"The Portuguese community has been a relatively undocumented group," said Sousa, himself an immigrant from the Azores, a Portuguese archipelago. "I thought this was a fantastic opportunity to document that history and make it available not only to Portuguese-Americans but to anyone interested in their story or immigration history."

At the beginning of the twentieth century, New Bedford was the town with the largest Portuguese population, counting 7,300 first-generation Portuguese parentages. The total constituted 16 percent of the city's population.

As the Portuguese community began to increase in population, it established the first Portuguese parish in the city, St. John the Baptist (1871).

Since 2009, the city has been home to the **New Bedford Bay Sox** baseball franchise of the New England Collegiate Baseball League, a collegiate summer baseball league operating in New England.

New Bedford's **70 textile mills** made it the wealthiest city per person in the world — for the second time after whaling in the 1920s.

The Feast of the Blessed Sacrament is an annual four-day Portuguese cultural festival held at Madeira Field in New Bedford, Massachusetts. It is recognized as the largest festival of Portuguese culture in the world and the largest ethnic festival in New England.

The Feast of the Blessed Sacrament also has Madeira wine imported in casks from Madeira through an agreement with the Madeiran government.

The **Whaling Museum** has the skeletons of a 66-foot (20 m)-long baby blue whale (obtained in 2000), a 35-foot (11 m)-long adult humpback whale (acquired in 1900), and a 45-foot (14 m)-long sperm whale (obtained in 2004) on display. All whales died in New England waters.

The **Rotch-Jones-Duff House** and Garden Museum is a 28-room Greek Revival mansion built for the whaling merchant, William Rotch, Jr., in 1834.

Only one movie scene of *Moby Dick* was shot in New Bedford, and it was the scene in front of Seamen's Bethel. The scene was shot in 1956.

The **Seamen's Bethel** was specifically constructed for the many sailors who called New Bedford their home port (mostly whalers) and who considered it a matter of tradition to visit the chapel before setting sail.

The pew where Herman Melville sat at the **Seamen's Bethel** is marked when he visited in 1840. Bethel, which means "House of God," is a word from the Hebrew Bible.

Lewis Hine, in 1912 came to New Bedford to document the conditions in the mills for his work with the National Child Labor Committee. Hines and other reformers like Jacob Riis helped to change harsh child labor policies, which had allowed children under sixteen-years-old to work in dangerous and unhealthy conditions for more than ten hours a day.

All About Rochester

Rochester is a town in Plymouth County, Massachusetts. The population was 5,232 at the 2010 census.

Rochester was settled in 1679 on the lands called "Sippican" by the local Wampanoag tribe, along the coast of Buzzards Bay. (Sippican was the name of the local tribe) It originally included the lands of Mattapoisett, Marion and parts of Wareham (which was lost when Wareham was founded in 1739). The town was officially incorporated on June 4, 1686 as Rochester, and was named for Rochester, England, from which early settlers to the town came. The town originally thrived with the early shipbuilding and whaling trade in Mattapoisett Harbor. However, in 1852 and 1857 the towns of Marion and Mattapoisett, respectively, were separated and incorporated as separate towns, thus land-locking Rochester. Since that time, the town has become mostly rural-residential, with some farms located in town. Rochester is a "Right to Farm" community.

The original Joseph H. Plumb Library was established with a generous donation from Mrs. Charles Leonard in the late 1800s. Mr. & Mrs. Leonard resided at what is now known as Hiller Farm. The library was housed in the Town Hall until the 1970's.

The present library was built in 1976. The building and grounds were donated to the town by Dorothy (Gibbs) Bray Plumb, in memory of her late husband, Joseph H. Plumb who died in 1970. Joseph Hudson Plumb was born in 1913 and prior to living in Rochester, Massachusetts he resided in the neighboring town of Marion, Massachusetts. He was the son of Joseph Plumb and Maybelle Houghton. He wrote at least one novel, entitled *Trading West*, which was published in Boston by B. Humphries in 1940. It is a sea adventure story. Mr. Plumb was an avid boater, yachtsman, reader, and car collector. He and Dorothy Plumb lived in several of the prominent homes in Rochester. There are portraits of Mr. and Mrs. Plumb on display at the library, and Mr. Plumb's oversized, solid oak rocking chair is a favorite feature of the library's seating area.

People of Significance - Rochester

Joseph Bates (8 July 1792 – 19 March 1872) was an American seaman and revivalist minister born in Rochester. He was a co-founder and developer of Sabbatarian Adventism, whose followers would later establish the Seventh-day Adventist Church. Bates is also credited with convincing James White and Ellen G. White of the validity of the seventh-day Sabbath.

In 1793, Bates' family moved to the part of New Bedford, Massachusetts that would become the township of Fairhaven in 1812. In June 1807, Bates sailed as a cabin boy on the new ship commanded by Elias Terry, called the Fanny, to London via New York City. This was the commencement of Bates' sailing career. In 1811, Bates was forced into servitude for the British navy and spent time as a prisoner during the War of 1812. After his release he continued his career, eventually becoming captain of a ship.

He began a sailing career in 1807 as a cabin boy and continued into adulthood. During one of his voyages, he read a copy of the Bible that his wife packed for him. He experienced conversion and became involved in a variety of reforms, including helping to found an early temperance society. He became one of the champions of health reform; abstaining from all alcohol, tobacco, and caffeine, even becoming a vegetarian. In 1839 he accepted the teachings of William Miller that Jesus was coming soon.

After October 22, 1844, like many other Millerites, Bates sought meaning out of the Great Disappointment. During the spring of 1845, Bates accepted the seventh-day Sabbath after reading a pamphlet by T. M. Preble. Bates soon became known as the "apostle of the Sabbath" and wrote several booklets on the topic. One of the first, published in 1846, was entitled The Seventh Day Sabbath, a Perpetual Sign. One of Bates' most significant contributions was his ability to connect theologically the Sabbath with a unique understanding of the heavenly sanctuary. This apocalyptic understanding of theology would become known as the Great Controversy theme.

During the 1850s Bates supported the development of a more formal church organization that culminated in 1863 with the formation of the Seventh-day Adventist Church.

Bates' family home at 191 Main St., Fairhaven, MA was purchased by Adventist Heritage and is being restored as a heritage attraction.

Do You Know Rochester?

Rochester Memorial Day Boat Race is sponsored by the Rochester Fire Dept. The first race was held in 1934. The boat must be a homemade river racer design of any material, with two persons to a boat. There are no limitations or restrictions on types of paddles. Divisions include open/men's, women's, junior boys, junior girls, co-ed and parent/child. Junior division teams are with both contestants under 14 years old. Parent/child is for a parent with his/her child (child under 14 years old) or an adult (25 or older) with a child (child under 14 years old). Trophies are awarded to first, second and third place finishers in each division. A seminar about building a boat is available before the race.

With views of the Mattapoisett River and remnants of an old sawmill and settlement, **Church's Field** in Rochester offers lots to discover in its 32 acres. This property was in the Church family for nearly 400 years before the Rochester Land Trust acquired it in 2010 for conservation and outdoor exploration.

Farm to Fork Gourmet is the brain-child of Jody Amour, the former Executive Chef for the New England Patriots, Head Catering Chef for a Premier Catering Company in Metro West, and Executive Chef from the Beachwood Inn in Worcester, MA.

After an award-winning 20-year career in catering and food services, Jody saw the landscape of food changing and realized catering wasn't keeping up. As the demand for locally sourced and organic products increased, catering options basically stayed the same. Leaning on his unique approach to catering, he decided to do something about it and change the marketplace forever.

Rochester's pastoral landscape at **East Over Reservation**, a Trustees property next to Leonard's Pond and Eastover Farm is open to the public. Visitors to the reservation can amble through forests and fields that were once farmland and pasture. East Over's easy trails and rustic scenery make it a nice destination for a stroll any time of year.

All About Wareham

Wareham is a town. As of the 2010 census, the town had a population of 21,822.

Wareham was first settled in 1678 by Europeans as part of the towns of Plymouth and Rochester and incorporated in 1739 and named after the town of Wareham in England. Because of its geography, Wareham's early industry revolved around shipbuilding and the related industries. It also served as a resort town, with many smaller resorts scattered around the town, especially in Onset. Like Sandwich, its waterways, especially Buttermilk Bay, were considered as possible pathways for the Cape Cod Canal. Although the canal proper goes through Bourne and Sandwich, the southern approach to Buzzards Bay passes just south of the peninsulas that make up the topography of the town.

For years the town was known by its slogan "Gateway to Cape Cod," but in January 2020 adopted a new slogan: "It's Better Before the Bridges." The intent was to draw attention to the appeal of Wareham as a tourist destination itself, rather than as a conduit to somewhere.

The town has a total area of 46.3 square miles, of which 35.8 square miles is land and 10.5 square miles is water. The total area is 22.64% water.

Between the rivers and bays that make up Wareham lie several points and necks, including Cromesett Point, Swift's Neck, Long Beach Point, Indian Neck, Stony Point, Cedar Island Point, Codman's Point, Sias Point and Whittemore Point.

The town of Wareham encompasses a number of neighborhoods and named places including Onset, Wareham Center, West Wareham, East Wareham, and Weweantic.

There are a number of ponds and lakes in Wareham, including Blackmore Pond, Horseshoe Pond, and Mary's Pond.

People of Significance - Wareham

Samuel Thomas Wellman was born in Wareham, Massachusetts in 1847, died in 1919. Wellman was the son of a Nashua Iron Company superintendent. Wellman received his formal engineering training from Norwich University in Norwich, Vermont, and served as a corporal with the First New Hampshire Heavy Artillery during the Civil War. Shortly after the war, Wellman married Julia A. Ballard, with whom he had five children. He was an American steel industry pioneer, industrialist, and prolific inventor. Charles M. Schwab of Bethlehem Steel described Samuel T. Wellman as "the man who did more than any other living person in the development of steel" Wellman was a close friend of electrical pioneer George Westinghouse, and he was also president of the American Society of Mechanical Engineers from 1901 to 1902

Following an unsuccessful venture with his half-brother, Wellman later founded the Wellman-Seaver-Morgan Engineering Company in Cleveland, Ohio, which continues under a different name to this day.

Virginia Elizabeth "Geena" Davis was born January 21, 1956 in Wareham and is an American actress, advocate, executive producer, and former model. She is the recipient of several accolades, including an Academy Award and a Golden Globe Award, in addition to nominations for a BAFTA Award and a Primetime Emmy Award. In 2019, she was given the Jean Hersholt Humanitarian Award for the work she has done over the decades to fight gender bias on and off the screen in Hollywood.

Having graduated with a bachelor's degree in drama from Boston University in 1979, Davis signed with New York's Zoli modeling agency and started her career as a model. She made her acting debut in the film *Tootsie* (1982), in 1986 she starred in the thriller *The Fly* (1986), which proved to be one of her first box office hits.

In 2004, Davis launched the Geena Davis Institute on Gender in Media, which works collaboratively with the entertainment industry to dramatically increase the presence of female characters in media.

John Kendrick (1740–1794) was an American sea captain during the American Revolutionary War, nearly 60 years before U.S. Commodore Matthew Perry used gunboat diplomacy to force trade with isolationist Japan in 1853, Wareham's own Captain John Kendrick arrived on the island nation's shore.

Kendrick and his crew made landfall in Kushimoto giving him the likely distinction of being the first American official to meet the Japanese.

When he visited, Japan had been a closed nation for more than 150 years. During that time trade was limited to the Dutch, who were only allowed to dock one ship per year in Nagasaki. The strict policy kept foreigners out and the Japanese people isolated.

It would take more than sixty years before Commodore Matthew Perry appeared at Tokyo Bay.

Though born on Cape Cod, Kendrick settled his family in Wareham. The Kendrick house is located at 100 Main St. and houses a museum.

After Kendrick was killed by British cannon fire at Honolulu in 1794, his family remained in the house.

Eugene Thomas Maleska (January 6, 1916 – August 3, 1993) was a U.S. crossword puzzle constructor and editor.

The New York Times had published dozens of crosswords that he had submitted as a freelance contributor. He became the crossword editor for The New York Times in 1977.

Benjamin Spooner Briggs (April 24, 1835 – likely November 1872) was an experienced seaman and master mariner. He was the Captain of the merchant ship Mary Celeste, which was discovered unmanned and drifting in the Atlantic Ocean midway between the Azores and the coast of Portugal on December 4, 1872. The lifeboat was missing, yet the Mary Celeste herself was still under sail. Benjamin Briggs, his wife Sarah, and their two-year-old daughter Sophia Matilda were never found and are presumed lost, along with the crew of Mary Celeste.

Do You Know Wareham?

The **Wareham Historical Society** owns and maintains five important historical structures that represent an interesting sampling of Wareham's architectural history. The buildings are in the heart of Wareham's historic center and have a visible presence in town. They are: The Fearing Tavern Museum, The Old Methodist Meeting House, The One-Room Schoolhouse, The Union Chapel and The Capt. John Kendrick Maritime Museum

For those wondering where spiritualism rose from, it all started back in 1877 when a group of **Victorian Era Spiritualist** met on the shores of Onset Bay in Wareham and formed what is a modern-day center of American Spiritualism. However, the Onset Bay Center would soon collapse after two decades after the original group faced fraud allegations with claims that some of its mediums were a fraud. The influx of tourists looking for recreation as opposed to religious revelation also played a major role in its collapse.

A favorite spot for Onset locals is the **Wickets Island** that stands in the middle of Onset Bay. For beachcombing lovers, the eastside of the island is the perfect spot while those looking to relax can wade along the sandy beaches on the western side. With plans to open it as a picnic area, the Coalition is currently renovating the stone pier on the island to ensure visitors' safety.

There used to be a neighborhood known as **South Wareham** that was located where the current John. W Decas School stands. This neighborhood used to be in a world of its own-at least for people who grew up there. Life at South Wareham used to be rather predictable. Kids there went to school at Legion Hall while most of the adults worked at the Horseshoe Mill or the Beaton's Cranberry processing plant. Shoppers too would do their shopping at the Coyne's general store.

Water Wizz, touted as "Cape Cod's only water park", is a family-owned water park located in East Wareham, Massachusetts and attracting about 100,000 visitors yearly.

The park was used as a location in the 2010 film *Grown Ups* and the 2013 film *The Way Way Back*.

Wareham Sports are renowned for its powerful boys' basketball and football teams. The football team has won 6 South Coast Conference titles and has had 5 undefeated regular seasons (1978, 1980, 1995, 2004, 2006). They won the State Title in 1995, guided by All-American quarterback and linebacker, Stephen Cooper, played as an NFL linebacker for the San Diego Chargers. Wareham were also the State runners-up in 1980 and 2006. The Wareham football program has produced numerous Division 1 and NFL players, including Stephen Cooper (UMaine & NFL), Shea Allard (Delaware & NFL), Mike Laperriere (Northeastern), Wayne Sylvester (Kansas), and Darien Fernandez (Laramie - Wyoming).

The boys' basketball team is regarded as one of the best high school teams in New England. They won the 2009-2010 Division 3 State Championship. They have also compiled 4 undefeated seasons since 2002 and have competed in 5 Regional Championships and 3 State Championship games.

The color guard team has been the state champions in their division a total of three times. The years were: 2011 for their show "Glitter in the Air", 2012 for their show "Titanic" and 2014 for their show "Stormy Love".

Wareham is home to the **Wareham Gatemen**, an amateur collegiate summer baseball team in the Cape Cod Baseball League. The team plays its home games at Clem Spillane Field, and has featured dozens of players who went on to careers in Major League Baseball, such as Mo Vaughn, Lance Berkman, and Kyle Schwarber.

Many of the existing cottages in **Onset** were built as second homes for individuals from Boston, Taunton, Brockton and other northeastern cities who gathered to hear mediums communicate with the dead. While it was run by the Spiritualists, the village was known as Onset Bay Grove. Onset is a census designated place in the Town of Wareham.

What is this statue?

Answer on page 134

All About Westport

Westport was so named because it was the westernmost port in the Massachusetts Bay Colony. It was first settled by English colonists in 1670 as a part of the Town of Dartmouth by members of the Sisson family. The river, and the land around it, was called "Coaksett" in the original deed; the name, now spelled "Acoaxet," now refers to the southwestern community along the western branch of the Westport River.

Like many areas in the region, Westport was affected by King Philip's War, when the native Wampanoag population rebelled against the oppression of the English settlers. Several small mills were built along the Westport River, adding to its prosperity. In 1787, the growing town, along with the town of New Bedford, seceded from Dartmouth.

During the late 18th century, into the early 19th century, Paul Cuffee and his wife settled in the town. He was a Quaker businessman, sea captain, patriot, and abolitionist who developed a shipyard on the banks of the Westport River. Of Wampanoag and Ashanti ancestry, Cuffee became one of the richest free men of color in the United States at the time. He later helped the effort to resettle freed blacks to Sierra Leone in West Africa.

Several cotton mills operated along the river, the largest of which was at the junction of the river with Lake Noquochoke on the Dartmouth town line.

The Macomber turnip traces its ancestry to turnips sowed in Westport shortly after 1876.

During the Second World War, a coastal defense installation was raised on Gooseberry Island.

The town is now mostly residential, with a large farming community. Horseneck Beach State Reservation, located to the north and west of Gooseberry Island, is a popular summer destination for many in the area.

There are several unofficial localities within town: Head of Westport, South Westport, Westport Point, Central Village, North Westport (known in former times as Westport Factory) and Westport Harbor which is also often called Acoaxet, an early name. Because of the west branch of the Westport River, Acoaxet is inaccessible by land except by passing through Adamsville, Rhode Island.

Westport is a Right to Farm Community.

People of Significance – Westport

Thomas Church Brownell (October 19, 1779 – January 13, 1865) was founder of Trinity College in Hartford, Connecticut, and Presiding Bishop of the Episcopal Church from 1852 to 1865.

Brownell was born in Westport, Massachusetts on October 19, 1779. He was a descendant on his mother's side from Colonel Benjamin Church, an early settler in Little Compton, Rhode Island and the father of American ranging. He studied at Union College, Schenectady, New York, receiving his degree in 1804.

Brownell was ordained to the diaconate and priesthood by Bishop John Henry Hobart. He was consecrated Bishop of Connecticut in New Haven on October 27, 1819. Brownell's extensive writings include diocesan charges, liturgical material, scriptural commentaries and other works. He founded Washington College (now known as Trinity College), Hartford as a faith-based college and served as its first president for nearly a decade.

Brownell served as Presiding Bishop of the Episcopal Church from 1852 until his death, succeeding Philander Chase. Brownell was buried at Cedar Hill Cemetery, next to Samuel and Elizabeth Colt. Brownell had presided over their wedding in 1856.

Paul Cuffe or Cuffee (January 17, 1759 – September 7, 1817) was born free into a Native American—African American family on Cuttyhunk Island, Massachusetts. He became a successful businessman, merchant, sea captain, whaler, and abolitionist. His mother, Ruth Moses, was a Wampanoag from Harwich on Cape Cod and his father an Ashanti, captured as a child in West Africa and sold into slavery in Newport about 1720. In the mid-1740s the father was manumitted by his Quaker master, John Slocum, in Massachusetts and his parents married in 1747 in Dartmouth, Massachusetts.

A devout Quaker, Cuffe joined the Westport Friends Meeting in 1808 and often spoke at the Sunday services at the Westport Meeting

House and other Quaker meetings in Philadelphia. In 1813, he oversaw construction and donated half the money for a new meeting house in Westport that exists to this day. Very few people of color were admitted to the Friends Meeting in those years.

He became involved in the British effort to develop a colony in Sierra Leone, to which the British had transported many former slaves from America. Some were slaves who had sought refuge and freedom with British military units during the war. After the British were defeated, they took those freed slaves first to Nova Scotia and then in 1792 to Sierra Leone where they were settled in the new colony. At the urging of leading British abolitionists, in 1810 Cuffe sailed to Sierra Leone to learn what the conditions of these settlers were and whether he could help them. He concluded that efforts should be made to increase local production of exportable commodities and develop their own shipping capabilities rather than continuing to export slaves. Cuffe then sailed to England to meet with members of The African Institution, who were also leading abolitionists, and offer his recommendations for improving the lives of all the people in Sierra Leone. His recommendations were well received in London and he subsequently made two more trips to Sierra Leone to try to implement them.

On his last trip in 1815–16, he transported nine families of free blacks from Massachusetts to Sierra Leone to assist and work with the former slaves and other local residents to be more productive.

As one of the last surviving coastal farming communities in Massachusetts, Westport has a unique variety of landscapes, from the East and West Branches of the Westport River to neighboring farmlands, quiet woodlands, pristine beaches, and fertile marshes. All who know Westport appreciate these landscapes and their irreplaceable contribution to the Town's agricultural heritage, natural beauty, and traditional way of life.

In 1972, recognizing the vital importance of Westport's natural resources, and the need for community involvement in preserving them, a group of local residents formed the Westport Land Conservation Trust. Since then, the Land Trust has joined the efforts of various Town and State agencies to help many Westport property owners protect their land.

Do You Know – Westport?

Gooseberry Island draws an eclectic mix of families, boaters, dog walkers, birders, and outdoor enthusiasts. With strong, salty sea breezes and a stunning panoramic view of Buzzards Bay, the island is a destination for anyone who loves exploring the coast. Gooseberry Island is also home to a concrete observation tower that was built during World War II as part of the coastal defense system to watch for German submarines.

The island is connected to the mainland by the short Thomas E. Pettey Memorial Causeway. On the east side, Buzzards Bay laps gently along a sandy beach. There's an unimproved shoreline boat ramp here, which is best for kayakers, windsurfers, small skiffs, and other small watercraft because it's very shallow and surrounded by rocks.

Located in the east branch of the Westport River, these three **Westport Land Conservation Trust** (WLCT) owned islands are great destinations for a short day trip on a small boat or kayak. You'll find stunning views and island serenity on their sandy shores and bordering salt marsh. For a long walk, land on the northern edge of Lower Spectacle at low tide, where you'll find a long crescent of beach and numerous birds gathered on the island's sand bar. Though these hilly islands are forested, the WLCT has not created trails here, and asks that adventurers stay on the beach.

Donated to the Westport Land Conservation Trust in 1973, Big and Little Ram Island are made up of broad salt marshes near the mouth of the Westport River's east branch. The marshes are a familiar landmark for Westport boaters heading out into the Bay — but did you know they're also somewhere you can explore? Natural river channels and man-made dikes, carved for flood control in the previous century, run throughout the marsh and create a maze of waterways that are great for spotting marsh wildlife by kayak or canoe. This trip is for experienced paddlers who are comfortable using a compass, as the many channels could get you turned around.

The area referred to either as **"Acoaxet"** or "Westport Harbor," which is between the west branch of the river and Rhode Island. This area is cut off from the rest of Massachusetts by water and Rhode Island.

In the 1870's wealthy Fall River factory owners and professionals began to settle on large estates and summer colonies near the shore. The largest of these colonies, located near the southwestern corner of Westport, became known as Acoaxet. So physically and socially isolated was this group that in the 1920s, Acoaxet attempted to secede and form a new town.

The history of the **Acoaxet Chapel** is a story of Yankee thrift, practicality, and resoluteness. It is veined with an uncommon sense of inclusion that far predates the contemporary sense of ecumenism. It also reveals the sustaining importance of the church in the lives of the farmers and businessmen who made up Westport Harbor's population.

Farm families in the Harbor began meeting in each other's homes for prayer, singing, and religious instruction in the 1840s. Over time, sentiment grew for having a formal meeting place. In January 1872, with the nearest church four miles distant, Frank Howland spearheaded a successful effort to build a local chapel. One of the group's first acts was to form the "Free Chapel Association"; all in attendance became members. They wrote a constitution and ratified it.

By the time they broke ground on January 23, 1872, two things were abundantly clear to them. First, they would pay cash for everything and avoid debt by raising money within their own community.

Second, they decided unanimously that the chapel would be "held in trust for the free use of all Protestant denominations for the worship of God and for moral and religious instruction" for the community.

Bradford and Eileen Faxon frequent **The Back Eddy**, sometimes accompanied by their son, professional golfer, Brad Faxon.

Fishing in New Bedford

New Bedford's reign as the most valuable port in the country reached 19 straight years as NOAA released its report on U.S. Fisheries for 2018.

New Bedford and Dutch Harbor in Alaska continue to dominate the list of top ports driven by landings of top-valued sea scallops locally and pollock for Alaska — the nation's largest commercial fishery.

New Bedford brought in $431 million in 2018, up from $390 million in 2017, making it the top port by value in the country for the 19th straight year.

According to the Fisheries of the United States report, which is compiled by NOAA, U.S. highest value species groups in 2018 included lobster ($684 million), crabs ($645 million), salmon ($598 million), scallops ($541 million), and shrimp ($496 million).

The majority (80%) of the catch in New Bedford is scallops. As on a tree, each ring on a scallop shell marks a year of age. Most sea scallops are caught in about 150 to 250 feet of water. A significant part of the work on a scallop boat is shucking the scallops, all done by hand on New Bedford's boats, to remove the part that ends up on your table and throwing the shells and the rest of the scallop overboard.

Located in New Bedford at 39 Bethel Street, the New Bedford Fishing Heritage Center is devoted to preserving and presenting the story of the fishing industry past, present, and future through exhibits, programs, and archives.

The Center uses retired/former fishermen/workers as docents, advisors, and presenters, and it provides a gathering place for fishermen and others in the industry. The Center uniquely honors those lost at sea.

The Center is the place to learn or expand your knowledge about the fishing industry in New Bedford.

What is this boat?

What is this boat?

Answers on page 134

Folklore – Fishing

Every profession has their superstitions, traditional customs and strange beliefs but mariners (and specifically fishermen) have more than their fair share. Most are associated with bad luck and are portentous of ominous weather, tragedy or poor fishing. From the notion of women on board being a distraction to whistling on the bridge inciting a storm there are dozens of ways in which misfortune can be wrought upon a vessel or voyage.

Here are some of them.

Friday is considered unlucky in many walks of life and remains prevalent even in today's modern seafaring world.

Though most commercial vessels wouldn't delay a voyage that was due to start on a Friday, there are still plenty of fishermen who prefer to stay on dry land at the end of a week

The belief is thought to be linked to the fact that Christ was crucified on a Friday and voyages destined to leave for sea would have an unlucky voyage. In the same vein, Sunday's are a good day to set sail as Jesus was resurrected on the Sabbath.

In the nautical world, cats feature quite a lot and particularly with fishermen. Any fishermen heading off to sea would be only too pleased to attract the attention of a cat; one that purrs before a launch is said to bring a bountiful haul as will one that rubs itself against the ankles of the crew. The reasoning being a sound one; that cats can smell the fish a mile away.

A black cat on the deck of a ship of its own free will is considered good luck. However, many commercial fishermen claim that a cat carries a gale in its tail or can excite a storm by licking its coat the wrong way.

Interestingly, the enduringly charming curse, 'son of a gun' is derived from the activities of sailors who failed to stay focused on their activities. The practice of consummating an affair on board was often done so on the gun deck, sometimes resulting in a child born out of wedlock; a son of a gun. And it wasn't just females of our own species that were purported to have a distracting effect on history's mariners; mermaids were also renowned to lure vulnerable sailors to their doom.

Superstitious fishermen refer to small ripples on the surface of the ocean as "cat's paws," while a great disturbance of the water is called "cat's skin." Dropping a cake of ice overboard would ensure a big catch.

Spitting into the mouth of the first fish you catch was also believed to improve the haul of the day. It was generally held to be true that letting the skipper spit into the water ahead of him would drive the fish away.

No bananas on board, bananas were thought to be terrible bad luck for a vessel. The superstition resulted from observations that those vessels carrying bananas as cargo befell some strange and unusual fates. Some ships simply disappeared whilst others suffered outbreaks of mysterious illnesses among the crew resulting in sickness and sometimes death.

The popular phrase, "whistling up a storm," derived from the commonly held belief that whistling whilst on the bridge would result in the onset of strong winds.

Clapping too could also be blamed for inciting lighting and thunder whilst throwing a penny overboard would bring a favorable wind.

Birds are not necessarily a fisherman's friend. Dreaded is a crow flying across the bow.

Never board a fishing vessel with a suitcase or wearing gray gloves: All hands may be lost

Cranberries

The Pilgrims discovered cranberries growing wild in bogs near their settlement in Plymouth and christened them "crane berries" because their spring blossoms resemble the shape of the shore bird's head and beak. From their Native American neighbors, the Pilgrims learned to use cranberries not only for food and medicinal purposes but as a natural dye. Cranberries are one of only three fruits native to North America that are now cultivated commercially. Like blueberries and Concord grapes, demand for cranberries has escalated worldwide as knowledge of their nutritive properties has increased.

When radiant red cranberries percolate to the surface of a flooded bog, it is quite a sight. When bogs are flooded using a sprinkler irrigation system, naturally buoyant cranberries wriggle themselves loose from their vines and pop to the surface. Wind propels the berries toward one corner of the bog, and a boom is used to corral the cranberries toward a pump truck or conveyor system on shore. Rocky Maple Bogs (18 North Carver Road, Wareham) is worth a drive-by if you're hoping to stumble upon a scene like this during cranberry season.

The cranberry beaters, sometimes called "eggbeaters," you may get to see in action don't actually pluck cranberries. Their paddle wheels agitate the water, coaxing reluctant cranberries to release from the vine. Once a bog is flooded, cranberry harvesters work against the clock to get the product out of the bog and to the processing plant before berries spoil.

The A.D. Makepeace Company, based in Wareham, is the world's largest cranberry grower, the largest private property owner in eastern Massachusetts, and a recognized leader in environmentally responsible real estate development and stewardship. Its 160-year history in the cranberry industry strengthens the communities they build. Makepeace Farms is a country market on the farm offering fresh baked goods, made to order sandwiches, fresh salads, cranberry products, and a variety of local products.

History of the American Cranberry

The cranberry is a native American fruit. The plant is a low-growing, trailing, woody vine with a perennial habit. Cranberries produce stems or runners from one to six feet long. During the growing season, the leaves are dark green and glossy, turning reddish-brown during the dormant season. The vines form a thick mat over the surface of a cultivated bed.

Short vertical upright branches, known as uprights, form from the buds along the runners. The uprights have a vertical (non-trailing) growth habit and form the terminal buds that contain the flower buds. Most of the fruit is formed from the flowers on the uprights, with some berries arising from flowers on the runner ends.

The plants thrive on the special combination of soils and hydrology found in wetlands. Natural Massachusetts bogs evolved from glacial deposits that left kettle holes lined with impermeable materials. These kettles became filled with water and decaying matter, creating the ideal environment for cranberries. Growing cranberries commercially also requires a surrounding network of support acres – the fields, forests, streams, and ponds that make up the cranberry wetlands system.

Cranberry bog soil is unique in that it consists of alternating layers of sand and organic matter. Dead leaves accumulate over the course of time and sand is added to the bed surface every 2-5 years to encourage upright production and maintain productivity.

UMass Cranberry Station

Notable South Coast Women

Introduction

I have selected just a small sample of the women who have made significant contributions to the formation and success of the communities of the South Coast. I know there are many more but information is not readily available about many.

Awashonks was a Native American woman who served as a chief of the Sakonnet people who lived in the southwest corner of Plymouth Colony. She was the wife of the Sakonnet sachem Tolony and became sachem at his death. She was born around 1640 and died sometime after 1683 when her name last appears in a court case.

In 1671, Awashonks was a signer of a peace agreement between a confederation of local tribes and Plymouth Colony. She became an important player in King Philip's War of 1675-76 as the English colonists worked to divide the Native tribes in Massachusetts, Rhode Island, to stop support of Metacom (King Philip). Strategically switching sides to safeguard her people from enslavement, forced labor practices and banishment to slave colonies, Awashonks initially supported Chief Metacom, her cousin. However, when he broke the treaty in 1675, Awashonks had already made peace with the settlers and switched sides.

Awashonks' bargain with the English initially protected the Sakonnet people immediately after the war, but their land was taken and its people did suffer displacement and enslavement.

Margaret A. Duggan Ryckebusch (1940-1998) was born and grew up in New Bedford. Her father, a prominent lawyer became New Bedford's City Solicitor, and later was Assistant Attorney General under

Democratic President Harry S. Truman. During his tenure the family met many politicians, and throughout her life Margaret was politically active.

Margaret graduated from Sacred Heart Academy in Fairhaven, MA. She received her undergraduate degree from Stonehill College and her master's degree from Boston College. In 1968 she accepted a position as a professor in the English Department at Bristol Community College (BCC). She later became chair of the Department of Modern Languages, Fine Arts, and Humanities, where she developed its speech curriculum.

A 20-year union leader, Margaret served as chapter president of the Community College Council from 1982-1986. Beyond BCC, Margaret helped to create a Union Leadership Certificate program at University of Massachusetts, Dartmouth

Margaret was a dedicated teacher who challenged her students, holding them to high standards. She made connections, supporting students who were outside the mainstream society. She knew that all students had potential.

Before Margaret retired in 1998, she took a sabbatical to research bringing a sign language certificate to BCC. Her interest created the Deaf Studies program at BCC. In 2001 Margaret was memorialized in a mural, entitled for the impact she made, which is located in the historic district of New Bedford.

Rosalind Poll Brooker graduated from Boston University School of Law in 1952, and she returned to New Bedford to practice law. Rosalind began her life of public service in 1969 when she was elected as a member of the New Bedford City Council, eventually serving as president.

Mayor John Bullard appointed Rosalind as New Bedford's first woman City Solicitor. She became active in Republican politics, and was a confidant to state and national politicians, including U.S. Senator Edward Brooke. Governor Francis Sargent appointed her as Administrative Law Judge and Governor Michael Dukakis reappointed her to that position. In 2005, a public meeting room at New Bedford City Hall was named in her honor.

Rosalind was a trailblazer for women in the fields of law and politics. She is remembered as an intelligent leader committed to advancing women attorneys. She overcame every obstacle to make her community a better place.

Rosalind was married to Samuel S. Brooker and she moved to Naples, Florida in her retirement living there for 28 years. Rosalind died in 2016 and she is buried at Tifereth Israel Cemetery in Dartmouth. Rosalind rose up throughout her life and brought other women up with her.

Sarah Delano (1904-1994), was born in Chicago. She summered on the South Coast area with her grandmother, who owned a cottage in Nonquitt, South Dartmouth. She attended Vassar College, graduating in 1925. Sarah was married 3 times. Her second marriage was to New Bedford artist Clifford Ashley. Together they restored a Westport farmhouse and Sarah's interest in local architecture grew.

In 1951, *Sarah married New Bedford native Stephen C. L. Delano, one of the fo*unders of the Waterfront Historic Area League (WHALE). WHALE's first focus was preserving the waterfront. Sarah became WHALE's president (1966-1982). As president, in the early 1970's she fought the location of the new Route 18 through historic New Bedford, saving most of the waterfront, and more. Under Sarah's leadership, the Waterfront Historic District eventually became the New Bedford Whaling National Historical Park.

Sarah steered the process of revitalizing a deteriorating vaudevillian theater, and transforming it into today's Zeiterion performing arts center. Sarah also directed the renovation of an endangered Greek Revival whaling mansion, the William Rotch Jr. House, which became the Rotch-Jones-Duff House & Garden Museum.

In 1985, in her husband's memory, Sarah donated 110 acres of woodland in Rochester, MA to the Wildlands Trust to preserve the town's rural landscape and biodiversity.

The Sarah R. Delano Preservation Awards are given annually to individuals or groups.

Sarah's funeral services were held at the Zeiteron in 1994. Its lobby was dedicated to Sarah in 1999.

Artist **Elizabeth Terry Delano** (1845-1933) was born in Fairhaven. Her father was a first cousin of President Franklin Roosevelt's grandfather, and their ancestors had emigrated to America in 1621.

Elizabeth began painting as a small child, and devoted her life to painting. She studied in New York and Boston, and with noted portrait painters, William Merritt Chase, J. Alden Weir, and other famous artists.

Elizabeth held exhibitions at her Fairhaven studio and taught painting classes. Working mostly in oil, she painted familiar subjects – flowers, fruit and portraits. Among some of her noted portraits were those of Theodore Roosevelt and his son Quentin, John I. Bryant, Miss Melora Handy, and Mrs. John Coggeshall. Her most ambitious projects were large friezes painted for the homes of her cousin Warren Delano, Jr., each containing hundreds of chrysanthemum blossoms.

Involved in political issues, Elizabeth was a staunch supporter for Republican causes. The proceeds of her 1918 exhibit in the rotunda of the New Bedford Free Public Library were used to purchase liberty bonds. Throughout her life she worked for causes she felt were right. She chaired the arrangements for the National Woman's Party to speak in Fairhaven, later writing to urge Congress to grant full suffrage to women.

As Elizabeth aged her failing sight and health forced her to abandon the art work that she loved. She died in her 88th year while residing in Fairhaven's King's Daughters' Home.

Born in New Bedford, **Gladys Heuberger Sherman Ellis** (1916-2011) was one of 10 children, a lifelong resident of Mattapoisett and the first in her family to graduate high school. She had dreamed of attending Pratt Institute in New York, but there was no money. She was a self-taught artist, seamstress, needle worker, upholsterer, furniture refinisher, scrimshander and basket maker.

Gladys designed and created the Mattapoisett Basket, a unique regional form of the Nantucket Basket. Typically, the purse was an oval basket with a hinged clam-shell style top, an ivory closure, and handles attached at sides with ivory bolts. Gladys added carved ivory panels to the top and sides depicting home, family and Mattapoisett landmarks on scrimshaw panels.

For decades, Gladys taught basket making in her home at 87 North Street. Gladys also taught for over 25 years in the adult education program at Greater New Bedford Regional Vocational Technical High School. She was a faculty member at the annual Stowe Basketry Festival in Vermont. Gladys became known as a patient teacher, a perfectionist with an eye for detail and an enthusiasm for complex design.

Gladys was selected for inclusion in Early American Life magazine's Directory of Traditional American Crafts as one of the best artisans in the United States. A 1984 Gladys Ellis Mattapoisett Basket can be viewed on the website of the Boston Museum of Fine Arts. Gladys died on January 9, 2011 at the age of 94.

Helen Elizabeth Ellis began crafting people and animals for a dollhouse, as early as four. At the age of 12, Helen moved to Boston, where she attended Miss Ingalls' School in Cambridge, and learned woodworking, then attended Milton Academy. She returned to Boston to teach woodworking at the North Bennet Street School and the Child Walker School of Design. In 1909, Helen began teaching at Milton Academy, where she worked for 19 years.

In 1916, Helen bought a house on Main Road at Westport Point and opened the Whaler Tea Room. In 1928, Helen opened The Whaler Book Shop in a rented house on School Street. The book shop sold books, offered programs, and a circulating library. In 1930, she started a traveling bookstore, the Whaler on Wheels, but after six years, the bookstores closed due to the Great Depression

She was hired by the Old Dartmouth Historical Society, and in 1939, she became assistant curator, introducing exhibits of decorative arts and furnishings. In 1952, Helen combined her museum experience and her commitment to education to open the Children's Museum of Dartmouth, a free museum for children.

Helen's woodcarving gained increasing recognition. She exhibited her work in New Bedford, New York and Boston (1932-1951), and she was elected to the National Association of Women Artists and Sculptors.

Helen died in Westport at the age of 89 on April 15, 1978. Her sculptures and personal papers were moved to the Old Dartmouth Historical Society, where they remain today.

Community advocate **Mary Santos Barros** (1923-2018) was born in New Bedford on December 26, 1923 to Jose and Julia Santos, natives of Sao Nicolau, Cape Verde. She was educated in the New Bedford school system through the technical school. As a teenager Mary did domestic work. She attended the University of Massachusetts Amherst and received a certificate from the Massachusetts Institute of Technology (MIT) for participating in the Community Fellows Program oriented by Boston activist Mel King.

On July 10, 1960 Mary was married to Jeronimo R. Barros, a native of Boa Vista and a lifelong mariner. In addition to raising their children, she worked in local factories for 31 years. Mary's concern for her own and other children led her to becoming an advocate for equal education for all children. She was active in the Parent Teacher Associations (PTA) at her children's schools, including T.A. Greene Elementary School, later renamed as the Mary S. Barros Educational Center. Mary often served as president of these PTAs. When she officially retired from work, Mary was employed by the Massachusetts Department of Social Services.

She served on the executive committee of the Committee of Concerned Parents for New Bedford schools and was instrumental in the building and naming of the Alfred J. Gomes Elementary School, named for a Cape Verdean attorney and leader. It was dedicated on October 27, 1977. She became a voice for Cape Verdean parents, often taking immigrant parents to school committee meetings and interpreting for them. She was a member of the Board of Education for the Commonwealth of Massachusetts from 1975-1979. She was recognized by them "for her distinguished service through the establishment of increased opportunities for the youth and exemplary parent participation." This was one of many awards that Mary received in her lifetime.

On the home front, Mary was the director of ONBOARD, the local anti-poverty agency, and a founding member of the Greater New Bedford Community Health Center. She worked tirelessly with the New Bedford Women's Center and with the NAACP in many capacities, including promoting the hiring of Cape Verdean bus drivers in the city of New Bedford. Mary was a dedicated parishioner at Our Lady of the Assumption Church, the first Cape Verdean Catholic church in the United States, of which her father was an original founder in 1905. Mary sang in the choir and represented the church at the National Black Catholic Congress. A woman of strong faith, her door was always open to anyone who had a problem.

In New Bedford, Mary belonged to the Martha Briggs Educational Club, which promotes advanced education for girls of color; the Cape Verdean Veterans Association Women's Auxiliary (the Cuckoo Club), which provided traditional Cape Verdean dance; as well as the Merchant Mariners' Social Club and Auxiliary. She was a member of the Cape Verdean American Federation and on the board of directors of TCHUBA, the American Committee of Cape Verde, which promoted Cape Verdean independence, achieved in 1975. Mary was a strong supporter of the revitalization of the Schooner Ernestina, a sailing ship that brought thousands of immigrants to the United States throughout the 20th century. A believer in political empowerment, Mary helped many people become American citizens. Mary's love of Cape Verde was as recognized in the archipelago as it was in the states. Having traveled to Cape Verde many times, she became more aware of the needs and the strengths of the land of her parents. Mary lobbied on behalf of Cape Verde on the state and federal levels. When natural disasters assaulted her family's homeland, Mary worked with others to raise funds and send needed supplies to the people of Cape Verde.

Consistent with Mary's deep commitment to New Bedford, she recognized that in order to accomplish certain objectives, one has to be politically involved on many levels. Mary was elected to the New Bedford City Council for two terms as Ward 4 councilor. She also was elected as a city and then a state Committeewoman to the Democratic Party Conventions. Mary was a strong advocate for all people, particularly people of color, including Cape Verdeans.

Mary died on November 14, 2018. Her legacy is the powerful example she role-modeled for her children and all community members, as she spread the knowledge that they can empower themselves as well as strengthen the community. By working together and recognizing that diversity is our strength, Mary taught us that we can build an inclusive community that treats all people with dignity and respect.

Folklore

Folklore – Acushnet

In Acushnet, a homeowner reported in 2016 that she heard whispering on a baby monitor in her son's room. She learned that her house had once been Kirby's Funeral Home. She's also heard children's voices and seen shadows, and psychics, mediums and paranormal investigators have visited and they reported hearing and seeing spirits and ghosts, she said.

Folklore – Fairhaven

During the Revolutionary war, Major Israel Fearing lead 100 men to Fort Phoenix to help drive British troops away from the Fort. His spirit is associated with the Fort especially relating to the sounds of cannon fire. It has been reported that people had seen a ghost jogging and stopping people to ask them for the time, only to disappear while they looked down at their watch.

The youngest daughter of Henry Huddleston Rogers, Millicent was buried in the foundation of the library that is named after her. There have been alleged sightings of a woman walking in the hallways, surrounded by a blue light. People also have reported seeing a woman in the windows of the tower, a section that is closed to the public.

Folklore - Fall River

In the Oak Grove Cemetery in Fall River where Lizzie Borden is buried, some have reported seeing strange lights at night.

The old ice house on Interlachen Island in the North Watuppa burned to the ground in 1933. Since then, some visitors report seeing large dogs and some claim to have been chased away by an unknown presence.

Some visitors who were visited Battleship Cove have claimed to hear voices in the narrow hallways of the World War II era warship battleship, the Massachusetts and others have reported a general feeling of being watched.

Lizzie Borden's home in Fall River is said to be haunted. Visitors have heard sounds of a woman weeping, seen lights flicker and even had a ghost in Victorian garb tuck them in when it was being used as a bed-and-breakfast.

The Freetown-Fall River State Forest is known as one of the most supernaturally active forests on Earth. It's part of the Bridgewater Triangle, an area of about 200 square miles with high levels of reported ghostly and unexplained activity. Visitors to the forest attest to spotting floating light orbs, giant snakes, UFOs, ghosts and strange small people darting between the trees. The forest is also the location of several documented murders, suicides and animal mutilations.

First, back to May of 1831. Historian Stefani Koorey, in her book "Historic Fires of Fall River," states that Hannah Borden Cook was digging in a sandbank at what is now Fifth and Hartwell streets. She needed sand to use as a scouring agent for spring cleaning. She found more than she bargained for: She uncovered a human skull.

The site was excavated. Diggers found the intact skeleton of a man, wrapped in bark and bark cloth. The man wore a brass breastplate and a belt of brass tube, and was carrying arrows tipped with brass arrowheads.

The skeleton and armor were moved to the Fall River Athenaeum and then lost in the fire of 1843 that took much of downtown.

Many believe it was the remains of a Wampanoag Indian Chief but there is no definite explanation as to the identity of the skeleton.

In 1903 a plaque was placed on the building commemorating the skeleton. In 1918 it was stolen but quickly found by the Fall River Police. A new plaque was placed higher on the building and now covered by a camera.

Folklore – Marion

William S. Moore, a veteran of the War of 1812, was appointed as the first keeper, at the lighthouse on Bird Island and the light went into operation on September 1, 1819.

A severe storm struck the area at the end of December 1819, devastating the new light station. Moore, who lost his boat and a large supply of wood, described the damage in a letter to Dearborn: It was reported that his wife died on the island but no grave was ever found.

But his wife did die on the island, and there are those who say it has been haunted or cursed ever since. According to legend some later keepers were frightened by the "ghost of a hunched-over old woman, rapping at the door during the night."

In 1872, Captain Benjamin Briggs (a native of Marion, MA)—along with his wife, two-year-old daughter, and crew of seven—set sail across the Atlantic on the brigantine merchant ship *Mary Celeste* to deliver a cargo of 1,701 barrels of industrial alcohol to Italy. About a month after their departure, the Canadian brigantine *Dei Gratia* found her off the coast of Portugal, sailing haphazardly with her sails torn. What they discovered upon boarding was a seemingly seaworthy ship, good supplies of food and fresh water, the crew's personal possessions, but not a trace of a single person.

The last entry in her ship's log was dated 10 days prior to the date she was found adrift. The ship's only lifeboat was missing, and one of its two pumps had been disassembled. Three and a half feet of water was sloshing in the ship's bottom, though the cargo of alcohol was largely intact. There was a six-month supply of food and water—but not a soul to consume it. A frayed line was trailing in the water behind the ship, and nine barrels of the alcohol were empty.

Folklore – Mattapoisett

At the Inn on Shipyard Park guests have reported seeing a sea captain looking out to the sea in one of the bedrooms. As well, a ghost named Sarah reportedly wanders the hall looking for her father.

Wolf Island Road in Mattapoisett. Legend has it that Colonial settlers killed some Wampanoag tribe members by hanging them from the nearby trees, and drivers report seeing the eyes of the dead men looking out from the trees especially in mid-summer. Also, according to local legend, a young man died in a car crash along this road 1970s, and if you park in the crash site and flash your headlights three times, his ghost will appear.

Folklore – New Bedford

Professional Ghostbusters deployed with the paranormal investigation team in 2005 to debunk claims that the city Armory is haunted. The mission in November as episode 107 of "ghost hunters" one-hour weekly TV series on the sci-fi channel. At the request of the National Guard, ghost hunters set up the command center in the empty Armory and began searching for reasonable explanations of the mysterious happenings. They had been on the job for three hours when nearing midnight, they entered into the gymnasium of the castle like fortress on Sycamore Street. The soundman was knocked to the ground, claiming he felt cold and something from the ground pulled him backward. He quit after filming that episode.

Folklore – Rochester

There is a large ivy-covered rock with witch painting on it. It is reported that witch's laughter coming out of cracks in rock. Supposedly site of the murder of a Salem woman who escaped the witch trials. The rock is located on private property under a tree at 1 Vaughn Rd. in Rochester.

Folklore – Wareham

Pukwudgies are creatures from Wampanoag oral tradition. They are said to be tiny, humanlike creatures that inhabit the swampy regions eastern Massachusetts. They are described as tricksters with smooth, grey skin and the ability to appear and vanish at will.

Fearing Tavern in Wareham dates back to 1660, it was owned by Major Israel Fearing, has been used as a tavern, courthouse, town hall, post office and private residence. These days, it is a museum refurbished back to its colonial style. Ghost hunters once heard an electronic voice phenomena saying "hey Ashford. I killed Grandpa, Ash, I just knew you'd feel the pain. Then you can consider it a gift."

Treasures of the South Coast

That special place or institution that generates good feelings and a sense of wonder by people who experience them. Some are well known, and others are known best by the locals. The South Coast has many of these. I have selected the ones that to me, and hopefully to the reader, qualify as a special place that imparts some knowledge and generates good feelings and that sense of wonderment.

I have visited each and sought opinions from a broad group of people, residents, and visitors to the South Coast. We who live on the South Coast are very fortunate to have so many unique places that qualify as "that special place or institution." They are:

Acushnet

Step back in time at **White's Factory**, the ruins of a former cotton and sawmill along the edge of the freshwater Acushnet River. These stone walls have stood for over 200 years at this former hotspot of the local industry. Today, this conserved property protects clean water and river habitat for migratory fish.

White's Factory is named for William White Sr., who first built a water-powered cotton mill on this site in 1799. The mill, which one of the first cotton-spinning mills in the nation, provided most of the jobs in Acushnet outside of farming. It remained in operation until 1854 when the owners converted it to a sawmill that ran into the 20th century.

After it was abandoned, the former mill became covered in plant growth until volunteers restored the ruins in 2008. Today, the walls and water wheel arches of White's Factory are a popular draw for photographers who love to use these ancient-looking stones as a backdrop for portraits or contrast them against the dramatic open sky beyond. If you're exploring the ruins, take care around its old stone walls; they are unsupported and could collapse if climbed or pushed on.

Two acres are protected by the Fairhaven-Acushnet Land Trust stretch behind White's Factory. Picnic tables are located behind the ruins and down by the riverbank.

Dartmouth

Cornell Farm is a beautiful historic farmstead property overseen by the Dartmouth Natural Resources Trust, maintained as an ecological and educational resource for the greater Massachusetts community. The same family held the farmstead for more than 150 years, located within an area of stunning natural beauty containing mixed forest, cultivated upland, and pristine salt marsh environments along the southern coast of Buzzards Bay. Visitors can explore the farmstead's preserved grounds and hike along gorgeous nature trails that meander through pine and oak woodlands and serene salt marsh habitats. The farmstead is open to the public year-round from dawn to dusk.

520 Smith Neck Rd, South Dartmouth, MA 02748

Padanaram is a coastal village in South Dartmouth. The village was one of many settlements that began cropping up within the town of Old Dartmouth after its purchase from the Wampanoag by members of the Plymouth Colony in 1652. During King Philip's War, the settlement was burned down, and all cattle were killed. The only settlers who survived were those who heard a warning and fled either to Russell's Garrison or Cooke's Garrison. Remains of the settlement can still be seen at the foot of Lucy Street. In the mid-18th century, it became a shipbuilding center. In September 1778, during the American Revolution, the British attacked nearby New Bedford with a small force attacking Padanaram unsuccessfully.

The town prospered as a minor whaling port and was home to a large salt works during the 19th century. As these industries died out, "the village" (as it is referred to by locals) became mostly a residential area with several yachting businesses, galleries, eateries, and shops. It is also home to the New Bedford Yacht Club.

"A great place to visit and wander around the shops, galleries, and restaurants and to view the boats in the harbor." -Henry Quinlan, author

Fairhaven

Fort Phoenix (now the Fort Phoenix State Reservation) is located in Fairhaven at the mouth of the Acushnet River, and it served, during colonial and revolutionary times, as the primary defense against sea-borne attacks on New Bedford harbor.

Within sight of the Fort, the first naval battle of the American Revolution took place on May 14, 1775. Under the command of Nathaniel Pope and Daniel Egery, a group of 25 Fairhaven minutemen (including Noah Stoddard) aboard the sloop *Success* retrieved two vessels previously captured by a British warship in Buzzards Bay.

On September 5 and 6, 1778, the British landed four thousand soldiers on the Acushnet River's west side. They burned ships and warehouses in New Bedford, skirmished at the Head-of-the-River bridge (approximately where the Main Street bridge in Acushnet is presently situated), and marched through Fairhaven to Sconticut Neck, burning homes along the way. In deference to the overwhelming force approaching from the landward side, the fort was abandoned, and the enemy destroyed it. An attack on Fairhaven village itself was repelled by the militia under the command of Major Israel Fearing, who had marched from Wareham, some 15 miles away, with additional militiamen. Fearing's heroic action saved Fairhaven from further molestation.

The Fort was enlarged before the War of 1812, and it helped repel an attack on the harbor by British forces. In the early morning hours of June 13, 1814, landing boats were launched from the British raider, HMS *Nimrod*. Alerted by the firing of the guns at Fort Phoenix, the militia gathered, and the British did not come ashore.

The Fort was decommissioned in 1876, and in 1926 the site was donated to the town by Cara Rogers Broughton (a daughter of Henry Huttleston Rogers). Today, the area surrounding the Fort includes a park and a bathing beach. The fort lies just to the seaward side of the harbor's hurricane barrier.

"The benches in the Reservation offer a soothing view of the ocean and on beautiful days, year round, will often be filled." *–Henry Quinlan, author*

All of the buildings donated by Henry Huttleston Rogers. They are the Fairhaven High School, the Rogers School, the Town Hall and Unitarian Memorial Church. A granite shaft on the High School lawn is dedicated to Rogers. In Riverside Cemetery, the Henry Huttleston Rogers Mausoleum is patterned after the Temple of Minerva in Athens, Greece. Henry, his first wife Abbie, and several family members are interred there.

In the **Millicent Library** of Fairhaven, Massachusetts, there is a spectacular window of stained glass. It is sixteen feet in height and was crafted in 1891 in London by the firm of Clayton & Bell. Within one of its compartments is depicted in gem-like colors a likeness of the great Shakespeare. To right and left in encircling frames are the names of American poets, but the lower and outstanding pane shows a female form — the gentle muse of poetry herself in softly draped robes — her face, pure and lovely, raised in a sort of adoration. The spectator knows at once that this is a real face, the actual likeness of a flesh and blood maiden. The face is that of Millicent Rogers, in whose memory the window was mounted — and, indeed, the whole building was raised.

Young Millicent Rogers was the daughter of H.H. Rogers oil tycoon, millionaire and generous benefactor in his home town of Fairhaven, Massachusetts. Millicent and her sisters and brother had been happy vacation and weekend habitués of the little town from birth, and with their parents, both of whom were themselves Fairhaven natives — had spent happy, care-free hours here among relatives and friends, in particular communion with both maternal and paternal grandparents.

The Riverside Cemetery was created in 1850 by Warren Delano II, the grandfather of President Franklin Delano Roosevelt, this is one of the most beautiful rural-style cemeteries in Massachusetts. It is the final resting places of some of the town's most prominent people. You'll also see lovely examples of early tombstone art as you walk along the beautifully landscaped paths.

Fall River

During the Depression, in 1936, the Federal One division of the Works Progress Administration commissioned artist **John Mann to create a mural** or series of murals depicting the history of Fall River.

John Mann studied the history of the city and, after four months of intense research, began to paint a chronological account of Fall River that spanned from the Native American tribes to the Cotton Industry era. Through the facilities of the Public Library and the Fall River Historical Society and with the cooperation of many of Fall River's oldest families, he was able to obtain much information concerning early Fall River history. Mann chose the subjects of the paintings at his discretion and, judging from the finished products; he succeeded in making fascinating choices. The murals were painted in the auditorium of the B.M.C Durfee High School Technical Building (later the Matthew J. Kuss Middle School and currently the Resiliency Preparatory School).

There are three sets of murals, each depicting a different era in Fall River's history. The first mural series contains six panels about Native American history. The second mural recreates Fall River's history from the Revolutionary War to the Civil War. The last mural centers on the history of Fall River in the cotton mill era.

"There are many examples like these that demonstrate the help that the government provided during the Great Depression. These are worthy examples." –Henry Quinlan, Author

There are five National Historic Landmarks and Official Veteran Memorials on both state and national levels, located within **Battleship Cove**. It has been providing the preservation of both the military heritage of the New England region and that of the United States since 1965. A non-profit memorial and Museum located in Fall River, Massachusetts, where veterans, families, schools, Scouts, and interested visitors worldwide have walked the decks of these historic vessels and viewed the legendary aircraft on display. Day visits, overnight camping experiences, and special events allow the public to immerse themselves in exploring the historic entities on exhibit. They experience for themselves the sacrifices made by both the military personnel who served on these great ships and aircraft and those who supported their construction. See battle-ship USS Massachusetts BB59, the destroyer USS Joseph P. Kennedy Jr DD850, submarine USS Lionfish SS298, PT Boats 617 and 796, and German missile corvette Hiddensee.

"Walking the decks and bowels of these ships gives the visitor a sense of the sacrifice so many have made for this country." –Henry Quinlan, Author

The **Kennedy Park** was originally the farm of John Durfee. The location gained national attention in December 1832, when the pregnant lifeless body of Sarah M. Cornell was found hanging from a stackpole there. Her death was later deemed to be murder. Methodist minister Ephraim K. Avery was accused of the crime, but acquitted after a sensational trial. The verdict outraged many local citizens. Sarah's body was initially buried on the Durfee farm, but moved years later to Oak Grove Cemetery when the park was being built.

Built in 1868, designed by famed 19th century landscape architect Frederick Law Olmsted and Calvert Vaux, the park was originally known as "South Park". It was updated in 1904 by the Olmsted Brothers. The park was renamed in 1963 following the assassination of President John F. Kennedy.

The park has three sections: a flat upper section used for baseball and recreation fields, a sloping middle portion with sweeping views of Mount Hope Bay, and a lower somewhat wooded portion along the Bay. The park was added to the National Historic Register in 1983. It was restored in 2001

Kennedy Park has long been used a place for public events in the city. In September 1996, over 25,000 people gathered in the lower portion of the park to see then President Bill Clinton during a campaign stop for his 1996 re-election.

Each August since 1986, the park hosts the Great Holy Ghost Feast of New England, a celebration of Azorean culture which attracts over 200,000 people each year. In 2014, an "inclusion playground" opened in Kennedy Park, which features equipment accessible to children with disabilities. The park includes a partially fenced playground area with slides, a seesaw, and mini monkey bars. An empty ice skating rink provides a place for children to ride bicycles.

Marion

The Marion Art Center (the MAC) is a dynamic non-profit organization offering a broad range of cultural experiences both in its historic building and across the community. The Marion Art Center's mission is to enrich the South Coast community by supporting and promoting a vibrant arts experience for all. It is well run by the current director Jodi Stevens.

The Center has two floors of gallery space where it hosts exhibitions for local artists. Artists have the opportunity to teach art classes.

Concerts at the Marion Art Center feature local musicians performing everything from Bluegrass to Bach in an intimate setting. Concerts are held in the beautifully renovated theater featuring an up-to-date, fully equipped sound system. MAC also presents four to five shows each year. In addition to comfortable theater seats, there is limited cabaret-style seating with audiences enjoying their refreshments at reserved tables.

"As a volunteer since 1970 and paid Executive Director 1985-2010 of the Marion Art Center, I know a lot about the Marion Art Center. For example, the building was originally a Universalist Church built-in 1830. By the 1940s, the church was abandoned. A group of volunteers (mostly actors and some artists) rented the space for $1 a year and fixed it up with all volunteer labor and local donations. All the hardware stores gave leftover paint, and they mixed all the colors to make "hardware gray," a color attempted to lovingly duplicate whenever repainting is done. Later through memberships and donations, the building was purchased and is privately owned and funded by the corporation of members.

I directed the popular play "Love Letters" by A.R. Gurney, using local celebrities and socialites to read the iconic piece. Geraldo Rivera was married to Marion's own C.C. Dyer at the time and agreed to donate his time (and personality) to participate in the fundraiser. On opening night, he asked, "what about the press?" We rarely got the press to show up for anything, but sure enough, at 7:30, the Channel 7 News truck drove up along with local reporters from New Bedford and the south coast! Our sold-out theater seats only 75 people, so I had to turn them away and received very negative reviews for my behavior! Geraldo was very kind." –Submitted by Wendy Bidstrup

Mattapoisett

Ned's Point is the site of a famous historic lighthouse that was built in 1837 in Mattapoisett. Ned's Point is also the site of a public beach that is popular with windsurfers. There are free parking and a restroom that is open on weekends during the summer season.

The town of Mattapoisett built the current Veterans Memorial Park surrounding the lighthouse as they received ownership of the land in 1958. They later petitioned to have the lantern relit, and the Coast guard granted their efforts in 1961.

"This is a great spot for a picnic or to just sit and enjoy the breeze and the view. There's plenty of parking, a nice gazebo, and picnic tables. A lovely spot." –Anonymous

New Bedford

The **New Bedford Whaling Museum** is a museum in New Bedford, Massachusetts that focuses on the history, science, art, and culture of the international whaling industry and the "Old Dartmouth" region (now the city of New Bedford and towns of Acushnet, Dartmouth, Fairhaven, and Westport) in the South Coast of Massachusetts. The Museum is governed by the Old Dartmouth Historical Society (ODHS), which was established in 1903 "to create and foster an interest in the history of Old Dartmouth." Since then, the Museum has expanded its scope to include programming that addresses global issues, "including the consequences of natural resource exhaustion, the diversification of industry, and tolerance in a multicultural society." Its collections include over 750,000 items, including 3,000 pieces of scrimshaw and 2,500 logbooks from whaling ships, both of which are the largest collections in the world, as well as five complete whale skeletons. The Museum's complex consists of several adjacent buildings housing 20 exhibit galleries and occupying an entire city block within the New Bedford Whaling National Historical Park. It operates independently.

The Museum also houses a collection of fine art, including works by significant American artists who lived or worked in the New Bedford area, such as Albert Bierstadt, William Bradford, and Albert Pinkham

Ryder, as well as a collection of locally produced decorative art, glassware, and furniture associated with the rise of New Bedford as a whaling port in the 19th century.

The Museum's Bourne Building houses the *Lagoda*, a half-scale model of a whaling ship that was commissioned in 1916 and is the world's largest model whaling ship.

The New Bedford Whaling Museum ignites learning through explorations of art, history, science, and culture rooted in the stories of people, the region, and an international seaport. The cornerstone of New Bedford Whaling National Historical Park, the Museum is located at 18 Johnny Cake Hill in the heart of the city's historic downtown.

"All in all, it was a huge highlight of our trip and appealed to all ages. A must-see if in the New Bedford area! If we are there again, we will return because there's so much more to soak up. The Whaling Museum may have been the best Museum of its kind we've ever been to!" **–Keena SD**

The mission of the **New Bedford Symphony Orchestra** is to place the world's finest music at the Center of the cultural life of the South Coast community. The NBSO enriches the lives of adults and children through the transforming power of great music, performing concerts at the highest level of professional standards and providing educational programs for children and listeners of all ages that deepen their enjoyment and understanding of music and make it a part of their daily lives.

The history and mission of the NBSO begin with its founder, Clarence Arey. In 1915, Mr. Arey, a gifted musician, and teacher established the New Bedford Symphony Orchestra to provide high-quality performances of classical music for his community. Mr. Arey also created the first public high school orchestra program in Massachusetts. When the New Bedford High School Orchestra performed at the annual Massachusetts Superintendents Conference in 1913, superintendents from around the state were so impressed with the quality of the performance that many of them returned home and quickly established orchestra programs in their school systems. Soon, almost every high school in Massachusetts boasted a student orchestra. Mr. Arey's dual devotion to a Symphony Orchestra presenting high-quality performances of classical music for its community and a music education program opening the world of classical music to young people remains the heart and soul of the New Bedford Symphony Orchestra.

NBSO's governance and management approach is rooted in strategic planning. Over the last fourteen years, the NBSO has completed four strategic plans. Each plan was developed to cover a three to five-year time frame to recognize that it is best to renew the process every three years. With this underpinning of strategic planning, the NBSO has experienced unprecedented growth. During this time period, the NBSO's budget has grown by a multiple of ten. The number of concerts presented has more than doubled, and educational programs have gone from serving 2,000 children annually to more than 8,000.

"If You Like Music" outreach approach, as described by David Prentiss on the Symphony's website, is one of the best outreach strategies I have seen."
-Henry Quinlan, author

On April 2, 1923, New Bedford opened its last new theatre in the city's downtown area – **The Zeiterion**. Built for the "live performance of vaudeville," it opened with "Troubles of 1922" starring and written by George Jessel. Barney Zeitz and his brothers built the $800,000 Zeiterion to be the biggest and best theatre in New Bedford. The two-story tapestry brick building, designed by Frank Leary and Frank Walker, is an adaption of the Georgian Revival style. Inside, the decorative shield with the family's "Z" logo and marble columned walls dominated the lobby. The Morning Mercury described the auditorium as "Impressive in its beauty." The color scheme was ivory and old rose; silk tapestry on the walls, a frieze of gold leaf Grecian dancing figures; a large oval sunset scene on the ceiling, an orchestra rail of solid gumwood, and a $7,000 cut glass Czechoslovakian chandelier.

The theatre did not meet with immediate success, and by September 1923, it had closed briefly and reopened that month as the STATE, a silent movie house. Its first film was the New England premiere of D. W. Griffith's *"The White Rose."* From this point on, the STATE would feature only occasional live performances.

Five world premieres were held at the STATE. The most important premiere was the 1956 opening of *"Moby Dick"* complete with Gregory Peck in attendance, a Time magazine souvenir issue, and a white whale that terrified audiences everywhere. The STATE was modernized in 1971.

Marble walls were covered with wood paneling, chandeliers in the lobby were removed, new rocking seats replaced original leather, and black paint replaced ivory and old rose.

On December 31, 1981, the theatre portion of the building was donated to the Waterfront Historic Area League (WHALE), who provided $200,000 for the first phase of restoration and commissioned a feasibility study.

Once one of 17 operating theatres in New Bedford, the Zeiterion, has been restored to its original grandeur. It is reborn as the symbol of an age when theatres were indeed palaces for the people.

The Zeiterion held its gala-reopening on September 25, 1982, starring Shirley Jones in Concert.

To become eligible for significant state funding for restoration, WHALE transferred the title of the theatre to the City of New Bedford. The building is now managed and maintained by The Zeiterion Theatre, Inc.

"I introduced my grandchildren to the wonders of live performances, and it has ignited their attraction to live theater." –Henry Quinlan, author

The **Buttonwood Park Zoo** is a seven-acre zoo located in the Center of Buttonwood Park. It is owned and operated by the City of New Bedford, with support from the Buttonwood Park Zoological Society.

The zoo opened in 1894 as a deer park and menagerie. In 1995 it was in deplorable condition and closed in 1998. It reopened in 2000 after major renovations. It is home to various North American wildlife, and it supports many conservation programs, such as the Cape Cod Stranding Network.

Approximately $7,000,000 in Capital Improvement Program bonds have been designated between 2014-2019 to update the facilities. Another $4,000,000 was funded by the Commonwealth of Massachusetts in 2018 for further improvements. It has been consistently noted as one of the best small zoos in America.

"There is not a better way for a young mother to spend a day with her children." –Sarah Murphy, Mattapoisett

The Wharfinger Building has a fascinating history. Between 1934 and 1935, the New Bedford economy was at an all-time low, but the city's fishing industry began to grow. Mayor Charles S. Ashley used WPA funds to demolish the Bristol, Acushnet, and Potomska textile mills and use the recycled bricks to construct several public buildings in the city. The recycled bricks from the Bristol Mill were used to build the Wharfinger Building on Pier 3. The Wharfinger Building was originally constructed to serve as the office for the city's "wharfinger," the individual who collected wharfage fees and oversaw other shipping activities of the port. During the winter months, the building was also used to provide shelter and warmth for women and children waiting to board steamships at the docks.

In 1941, the city opened the Wharfinger Building as the city's first official fish auction house. At the auctions, which began each day at 8:00 a.m., the entire catch of all participating fishing vessels was sold to the highest bidders in a matter of 15-20 minutes. In 1942, a one-story addition known as the "west wing" expanded the size of the building. As the city's fishing fleet landed more and more fish, this space was used to accommodate up to three auctioneers. In 1985, a bitter strike between fishermen and boat owners eventually caused the end of the daily auction, and instead, the private sales of fish became the norm. In 1994, the Whaling City Seafood Display Auction (now called BASE or Buyers and Sellers Exchange) was established. In 1997, this auction went electronic, and today it is the largest east coast seafood auction.

When the seafood auction ended, the City of New Bedford first used the Wharfinger Building to house offices for the city's tourism and marketing staff. About ten years ago, the Harbor Front Development Commission moved their offices into the original portion of the building. The west wing became the city's Waterfront Visitors Center, where today it continues to showcase the history and current status of the city's commercial fishing operations through exhibits and videos. Trained volunteers are available at the Visitors Center to answer questions and direct individuals to various waterfront activities and services, such as ferries providing transportation to the islands of Martha's Vineyard, Nantucket, and Cuttyhunk. Therefore, the construction project of the WPA remains in use today and still serves as a place to boost interest in the local community of New Bedford.

"This building ties in three great eras of New Bedford. The mill era, the fishing era, and today when New Bedford is emerging as a multi-dimensional economic community." –Henry Quinan, author

Rochester

The **East Over Reservation** is a 75-acre nature preserve and working farm managed by the Trustees of Reservations. There are hiking trails, quarry-stone walls, and a "treasure hunt" designed to test one's map reading skills. It was protected between 2003 and 2005.

East Over Reservation's agrarian terrain and iconic yellow farm buildings evoke a sense of days gone by. The old field habitat supports a distinctive assemblage of wildlife species, including blue-winged warbler, Eastern towhee, and cottontail rabbit. Two miles of quarry-stone-capped double walls surround it all and speak to the property's history: stone walls had become a more aesthetic element of rural architecture by the 19th century. The rock barriers surrounding the East Over landscape took more than a decade to complete.

Trails pass through a mosaic of farm fields, forests, and winding hedgerows. The surrounding woods shelter vernal pools, and, amidst the fields and barns, you'll find bobolinks, orioles, and chimney swifts.

Wareham

Wickets Island is a 4.6 acres island located in Onset Harbor in Wareham, Massachusetts. It is located 1,100 feet from shore.

The island is named for Jabez Wicket, a Wampanoag, who is said to have lived there in the late 18th century. The island was created during the end of the last glacial period and is a deposit of glacial moraine made up of coarse sand and soil that is a good producer of plant life but unsuitable for agriculture. A house occupied Wickets Island from the 19th century until it burned down in 1981.

In 2003, a developer purchased the island with plans to build a luxury home there. The Buzzards Bay Coalition purchased Wickets Island in 2016 as part of the developing Onset Bay Center, an on-the-water exploration center. The island is now permanently conserved and is being restored for public use for boating, paddling, quahogging, swimming, and beach exploration.

For beachcombing lovers, the eastside of the island is the perfect spot to visit while those looking to relax can wade along the sandy beaches on the western side. With plans to open it as a picnic area, the Coalition is currently renovating the stone pier on the island to ensure visitors' safety.

Westport

Horseneck Beach State Reservation is a public recreation area comprising more than 800 acres on the Atlantic Ocean in the southern portion of Westport. The reservation is one of the state's "most popular facilities welcoming hundreds of thousands of visitors per year." It is managed by the Massachusetts Department of Conservation and Recreation.

The reservation occupies a peninsula that juts out from Westport's mainland with Rhode Island Sound to the southwest and Buzzards Bay to the southeast. The reservation features 2 miles of barrier beach, marshland, and protected estuary habitat. Most of the marshland is concentrated at the northern portion of the peninsula bordering Horseneck Channel and The Let. The barrier island known as Gooseberry Neck (or Gooseberry Island) is connected by a causeway to the central peninsula and is the southernmost extension of Horseneck Beach State Reservation. It partially divides Rhode Island Sound from Buzzards Bay.

The name of the beach is believed to derive from the Algonquin word *hassanegk*, meaning "a house made of stone." Summer homes were built in the area after a bridge connected the beach to Westport Point in 1893. After all, were destroyed by hurricanes in 1938 and 1954, the state acquired Horseneck Beach in 1956. Gooseberry Neck was added to the state's holdings in 1957.

The state reservation offers fishing, windsurfing, motorized and non-motorized boating with boat ramp, trails for biking and walking, showers, hunting, and bird watching. The beach is located along the southern portion of the peninsula, bordering Rhode Island Sound and Buzzards Bay. Restroom facilities, management office, food bar, designated on-duty lifeguard towers, and paved walkways are found alongside the beach. A 100-site campground is located behind the dunes at Goose-berry Neck, at the eastern end of the reservation.

"This is a bang for your buck beach! A true local paradise. Facing the ocean, I walk far to the right. No lifeguards there, but I am cautious and aware of surf and rip tides." –Pamela, Dighton

As one of the last surviving coastal farming communities in Mas-sachusetts, Westport has a unique variety of landscapes, from the East and West Branches of the Westport River to neighboring farmlands, quiet woodlands, pristine beaches, and fertile marshes. All who know Westport appreciate these landscapes and their irreplaceable contribution to the Town's agricultural heritage, natural beauty, and traditional way of life.

In 1972, recognizing the vital importance of Westport's natural re-sources, and the need for community involvement in preserving them, a group of local residents formed the **Westport Land Conservation Trust**. Since then, the Land Trust has joined the efforts of various Town and State agencies to help many Westport property owners protect their land in keeping with its simple mission:

To acquire and preserve natural resources, farmland and wildlife areas for the use and enjoyment of present and future generations; to preserve and protect historic sites; to educate the public about the wise use of natural resources; and to work with other organizations having similar purpose.

Trivia Questions

1. Who were known during the Revolutionary War as the "fighting Quakers"?

2. What was the reputation of Onset in the 1950s?

3. What is "ghost gear"?

4. When was the lighthouse on Ned's Point built?

5. What did it cost to build the lighthouse on Ned's Point in 1838?

6. What are the Right-to-Farm communities on the South Coast?

7. What is a Right-to-Farm Community?

8. How long did it take to build the New Bedford/Fairhaven harbor barrier?

9. What Year was the Harbor Barrier built in New Bedford /Fairhaven Harbor?

10. What is the weight of each of the gates on the New Bedford Harbor Barrier?

11. How long does it take for each gate to close?

12. What was the name of the first whaling ship to sail from New Bedford?

13. What year was it built?

14. What famous act of defiance did the whaling ship *The Dartmouth* participate in Boston in 1772?

15. Were lobsters once considered a trash fish?

16. Where is Wharf Village?

17. What was the original name of Marion?

18. Why was Marion named after Francis Marion in 1852?

19. What island off the coast of the South Coast is connected to the land via a causeway?

20. What famous South Coast resident was once known as the "Witch of Wall Street"?

21. Why was Lizzie Borden's case a high-profile case?

22. Why was the Fall River Railroad Museum closed?

23. What are some of the amenities found at the Fall River Heritage Park?

24. Who started the Fall River Symphony Orchestra?

25. What is Fall River best remembered for?

26. Why was Lizzie Borden acquitted of her murder charges?

27. What started the Great Fire of 1843 in Fall River?

28. Where should you eat while at Fall River MA?

29. How many rooms were there in The Henry Huttleston Rogers mansion in Fairhaven?

30. What was the sale price when the Town of Fairhaven bought the mansion?

31. What is the new slogan for the Town of Wareham?

32. Where does the water of Onset Bay and Buttermilk Bay empty into?

33. What do these communities have in common? They are Onset, Wareham Center, West Wareham, East Wareham, and Weweantic.

34. Why was Route 28 in Wareham named the Cranberry Highway?

35. What is the name of Wareham's amateur collegiate summer baseball team in the Cape Cod Baseball League?

36. What is the name of the latest movie that was filmed at the Water Wizz in Wareham?

37. How many miles of coastline does the town of Wareham have?

38. Who built the first school in Wareham?

39. What was the original title of *Moby Dick*?

40. Who fist rendered whale fat that proved to be smokeless, scentless, beautiful lamp oil?

41. In the middle of the 19th century, where did London get the oil to fuel its streetlamps?

42. *Moby Dick* was a commercial failure until a famous author said: "I wish I had written that book." Who was the author and when did he say it?

43. Why was Westport so named?

44. On the morning of June 13, 1814, the British warship HMS *Nimrod* attacked what town in Massachusetts?

45. Henry Wadsworth Longfellow wrote a poem about Fall River, what was the title?

46. Who bought the first ticket to the premiere of the movie *Moby Dick* in 1956 in New Bedford?

47. The film premiered the film *Moby Dick* simultaneously at three theaters in New Bedford. What were their names?

48. In the fishing business what is a "nightrider"?

49. What does "shack" mean today in the fishing business?

50. In 1832 a skeleton was discovered in a sand bank near a church in Fall River. What was unusual about this skeleton?

51. How are fish lumpers who unload the catches on the docks paid?

52. At the height of the whaling industry in 1857, how many whaling ships were based in New Bedford?

53. When was New Bedford considered the richest per capita city in the world? 1930? 1812? 1857?

54. In what city is there a rainwater tax?

55. Why are some words pronounced different in Fall River than they are in New Bedford?

56. What is the distance between Fall River and New Bedford?

57. Where does the Quequechan River in Fall River empty into?

58. What does the phrase "daylight" the falls mean?

59. How did the great Fall River fire in 1843 begin?

60. There are three radio stations that serve New Bedford, two FM stations and 1 AM station. What are they?

61. There is an annual four-day Portuguese cultural festival held at Madeira Field in New Bedford, Massachusetts. What is its name?

62. Who organizes it?

63. What is the purpose of the Whaling City Festival?

64. Which brought greater wealth to New Bedford, whaling or the textile mills?

65. Who preceded the Portuguese immigration to the South Coast in the beginning of the 19th century?

66. Who followed the Portuguese?

67. The Ash Street Jail is noted for what?

68. There are two forts in Ft. Taber Park; what are they?

69. Hetty Green was nicknamed the "Witch of Wall Street." Hetty was said to be the richest woman in the world in her time, but she is listed as something quite different in the Guinness Book of Records. What is she called in the Book of Records?

70. Who greeted a crowd of 25,000 in Kennedy Park with "Obrigado Fall River!" on September 26, 1996?

71. What is the current use for the Borden Flats Lighthouse?

72. In Marion harbor there is something unique next to the Harbormaster's location. What is it?

73. There are tunnels that leave the waterfront and go uphill under what street?

74. In the 18th century they had these little cubicles underground which were areas used for protection against Indians, British

and other hostile forces. In what town were these cubicles found?

75. During the whaling days men were "shanghais." What does the phrase mean?

76. There is a beach located on Swifts Beach Road off Marion Road (Route 6), Resident, Non-Resident permit or a one-day pass required. What is its name?

77. Many say the tunnels under New Bedford were used for runaway slaves as part of the underground railroad. What were the other uses many suggested for these tunnels?

78. What is the origin of the name for Wickets Island in Onset Bay?

79. The Fairhaven-New Bedford Bridge is made up of 3 spans. What are they?

80. The Ice Cream Bucket is located on what beach that is open mid-May through Labor Day for ice cream and light fare?

81. What 1,800-foot saltwater beach is backed by rambling hills of beach grass and shaded, grassy picnic sites?

82. It really gives that "lost" feeling that keeps you from going to the other side of the island. If you do venture out, the island looks different from every point as you peruse its perimeter. What island is this?

83. What beach is located at the western end of Buzzard's Bay, the 2 mile-long beach is also great for bird watching?

84. What beach has outdoor showers, tennis courts, basketball court, picnic area?

85. What is the name of the beach in Marion that offers swimming and picnic areas and is open also to Rochester residents?

86. What were two of the former uses of the Westport Town Farm located at 830 Drift Road?

87. There are three radio stations that serve New Bedford. What are they?

88. There is an annual four-day Portuguese cultural festival held at Madeira Field in New Bedford, Massachusetts. What is its name?

89. Who organizes it?

90. What is the purpose of the Whaling City Festival?

91. Which brought greater wealth to New Bedford, whaling or the textile mills?

92. Who preceded the Portuguese immigration to the South Coast in the beginning of the 19th century?

93. Who followed the Portuguese?

94. The Ash Street Jail is noted for what?

95. There are two forts in Ft. Taber Park; what are they?

Trivia Answers

1. The owners in Dartmouth of eleven privateering vessels

2. A village of sin and corruption

3. Discarded or lost fishing gear

4. 1838

5. $5,000.00

6. Fairhaven, Rochester, Marion, Westport, Mattapoisett and Acushnet

7. Right-to-Farm laws protect farmers from lawsuits brought by neighbors who might be offended by the realities of farming operations.

8. Four Years

9. 1966

10. 400 tons

11. Twelve minutes

12. *The Dartmouth*

13. 1767

14. The Boston Tea Party

15. In the 19th century, lobsters were fed to livestock as well as the financially destitute, criminals, and indentured servants.

16. In Marion Center

17. Sippican

18. He was a Revolutionary War hero.

19. Gooseberry Island

20. Heddy Green

21. One of the factors that contributed to this case being high profile is because of the social status of Lizzie's larger family. The larger Borden's family was well known in Fall River as industrialists. The nature of her murders also played a part in the case at a time when women were rarely convicted.

22. The height of the popularity of the museum was between the 1990s and 2000s. A decade later, the number of visitors had declined significantly making it hard for the museum to pay its bills, hence the closure.

23. The park has an extensive boardwalk for wheelchairs, an antique carousel that was brought from Dartmouth's Lincoln Park, a 1.2 acres hay meadow that is perfect for picnicking and crafts fairs. Outdoor rock concerts are also common at the park.

24. The original orchestra was started by Messrs. Manuel Santos, who was a music professor on leave from Portugal, Bruno Pieroni, Manuel D. Perry and Louis Capanacci who were all violinists. The original founders then recruited other instrumentalists and had their first concert in 1926.

25. Fall River went from being a rural outpost to become the largest producer of textiles in the United States in the 19th Century. At the time, it was estimated that there were over a hundred textile mills in Fall River.

26. There was a no direct evidence linking Lizzie to the murders beyond any reasonable doubt. The major inconsistencies as well as a flawed prosecution process when presenting the evidence appeared to exonerate Lizzie.

27. The fire was started by two boys playing with a small cannon that subsequently ignited wood shavings that were near Borden Street. The high winds at the time fueled the fire and in no time, most of the buildings along Borden, Rock, Main and Franklin streets were engulfed in flames.

28. Having attracted immigrants especially from Portugal, Fall River is dotted with restaurants serving Mediterranean and Portuguese menus. Restaurants such as The Cove are popular

for their fish dishes and seafood. There is also the Caldeiras that is popular for its authentic Iberian flavors.

29. 85 rooms

30. $1.00

31. "It's Better Before the Bridges."

32. They both empty into the head of the bay, at the right-of-way of the Cape Cod Canal.

33. They are all located in Wareham.

34. Historically, the cranberry industry has dominated Wareham's economy, and one of the world's largest cranberry growers, the A.D. Makepeace Company (a founder of the Ocean Spray growers' cooperative), is headquartered in Wareham.

35. The Gatemen

36. *The Way, Way Back*

37. 54 miles

38. John Kendrick

39. *The Whale*

40. The Quakers

41. New Bedford whalers

42. William Faulkner, and it was said over 100 years after it was published.

43. It was the westernmost port in the Massachusetts Bay Colony.

44. Wareham

45. "The Skeleton in Armor"

46. Senator John F. Kennedy

47. State, Empire and New Bedford

48. A person who buys scallops for cash directly from a boat, usually at night.

49. Part of the catch taken by a member of the crew and sold for cash.

50. It was clad in body armor.

51. They get a small check and are then paid the remainder of their salary in cash. They often receive a bucket of fish on the side, which they are free to sell to fish markets or restaurants.

52. The harbor hosted 329 vessels worth over $12 million.

53. 1857

54. Fall River

55. Fall River was settled by people who had come to the area on steamboats from the New York City area to work in the textile mills. The accents have been in many cases carried down through the generations. That is not the case with New Bedford, where immigrants came more directly from Europe. Many of those who came to the Whaling City did so for the fishing industry.

56. 12 miles

57. Mount Hope Bay

58. To make them visible through restoration.

59. It happened when two boys playing with a small cannon set 20 acres of Fall River on fire, burning the post office, custom house, shops, banks, churches and the homes of 200 families.

60. FM stations WJFD-FM/97.3 (Portuguese-language) and WNBH-FM/101.3, and WNBH-AM/1340

61. The Feast of the Blessed Sacrament

62. It is organized by the Clube Madeirense S.S. Sacramento.

63. To raise money for scholarships and to raise money for local charities.

64. Textile Mills

65. The Irish

66. The French Canadians, the Polish and the Jewish community from Eastern Europe

67. The oldest continuing in-service jail in America. It has been in operation since 1829.

68. Fort Taber and Fort Rodman

69. She is listed in the Guinness Book of Records as the "World's Greatest Miser."

70. President Bill Clinton

71. It is an inn that accepts overnight stay for "Guest Light Keepers."

72. A small shellfish area that is stocked by the town

73. Rockdale Avenue

74. Dartmouth

75. A "shanghai" occurred when a drunken man was clubbed over the head and kidnapped through the tunnels. The poor souls caught in this situation were said to awaken at sea on a whaling ship and forced into labor.

76. Swifts Neck Beach

77. Bootlegging during prohibition, and smuggling

78. Jabez Wicket, an Indian and veteran of the French and Indian war, in 1795

79. The swing pan, Pope's Island to mainland Fairhaven, and mainland New Bedford to Fish Island

80. Apponagansett Park and Beach, 77 Gulf Road, South Dartmouth, offers scenic harbor views, a sandy beach area, gazebo for small functions, picnic area, volleyball court, playground equipment and basketball court.

81. Demarest Lloyd State Park, Barney's Joy Road, Dartmouth

82. West Island, Fairhaven

83. Horseneck Beach

84. Ft. Phoenix Beach

85. Silvershell Beach

86. During Colonial times the farm that served as a "poor farm" and infirmary for more than 100 years.

87. Two FM stations and 1 AM station. FM stations WJFD-FM/97.3 (Portuguese-language) and WNBH-FM/101.3, and WNBH-AM/1340.

88. The Feast of the Blessed Sacrament

89. It is organized by the Clube Madeirense S.S. Sacramento.

90. To raise money for scholarships and to raise money for local charities

91. Textile Mills

92. The Irish

93. The French Canadians, the Polish and the Jewish community from Eastern Europe

94. The oldest continuing in service jail in America. It has been in operation since 1829.

95. Fort Taber and Fort Rodman

Photos

Questions and Answers

What is it and where is it?

What is it and where is it?

Answers on page 134

What is it and where is it?

What is it and where is it?

Answers on page 134

What is it? Where is it?

What is it? Where is it?

Answers on page 134

Photo Answers

Page 76: This statue is a Civil War Memorial in Wareham.

Page 84, Top Photo: This boat is a new type of scalloper.

Page 84, Bottom Photo: This boat is a scalloper.

Page 131, Top Photo: The Stone House - The landmark house, located in Westport, was recently renovated by its owners. The house was built around 1830 at a cost reported to be $11,000. The stone used to build the mansion and the surrounding fence was thought to have come from a huge boulder (possibly an outcrop) on a farm a quarter mile away.

Page 131, Bottom Photo: The Tremont Nail Company was a nail manufacturing company located in Wareham from 1819 to 2006. The Tremont Nail brand was purchased by Acorn Manufacturing of Mansfield, Massachusetts, where it still produces cut nails and other products for restoration projects. They are the oldest manufacturer of steel cut nails in the United States.

Page 132, Top Photo: Pavilion in Kennedy Park, Fall River. View is of the Taunton River and across to Somerset and Swansea.

Page 132, Bottom Photo: Benches in Fort Phoenix Reservation in Fairhaven that look out toward the open harbor of New Bedford and Fairhaven.

Page 133, Top Photo: Cables and buoys that are taken out of the water and stored for the winter.

Page 133, Bottom Photo: These are cables that remain from the Marconi Towers that were built in Marion.

Many of the guy anchor foundations, which are 10-foot concrete cubes sunk in the ground, remain. In addition to the 14 400-foot tall guyed towers, an offshoot of fledgling radio company, Radio Corporation of America (RCA) installed three 245-foot tall, self-supporting towers for the station's new maritime communications mission in 1927.

You hear it before you see it. What is it?

Who is this? Where was it taken?

Answers on page 138

Where is this street?

What is it and where is it?

Answers on page 138

Where is this bench located?

Where is this?

Answers on page 138

Photo Answers

Page 135, Top Photo: The Quequechan River in Fall River. This is one of the few places you can see the River but remember if you go looking for it on Anawam Street you will hear before you see it.

The steep, western portion of the river between downtown and the waterfront originally consisted of a series of eight small waterfalls confined within a narrow, rocky bed. In the last half-mile the total drop is about 132 feet and the average flow is 122 cubic feet per second. The last 1,000 feet of the 2.5 mile length of the Quequechan River empties out into the end of the Taunton River at the head of Mount Hope Bay at Heritage Park making the total length of the Quequechan River at 2.7 miles.

Page 135, Bottom Photo: This picture was taken of President Franklin Delano Roosevelt when he spent a summer in Marion while he was taking a cure of his polio.

FDR sought Dr. McDonald's help in his own struggle with the polio and became both McDonald's patient and his friend. In 1925 and 1926, Roosevelt spent time on the Willibud Farm in Wareham so he could visit his doctor daily in Marion. According to information found in the Dr. McDonald recommended daily swims in Sippican Harbor off his own private pier, in addition to other water therapies that he devised specifically for Roosevelt.

Page 136, Top Photo: A Street in the National Whaling Historical District in New Bedford

Page 136, Bottom Photo: Replica of the Statute of Liberty located in Kennedy Park Fall River

Page 137, Top Photo: Waterfront walkway along western side of the outer New Bedford harbor. It abuts the Kennedy Memorial Highway. The view is of Fairhaven.

Page 137, Bottom Photo: Merchant Marine Memorial Walkway, New Bedford. Butler Flats Lighthouse in distance.

Who does this statute honor?

What is this?
Where is it located?

Answers on page 142

Where is this memorial garden and who does it honor?

What is this?

Answers on page 142

What was the original use of this building, 13 Marconi Way, Marion?

Where is this lighthouse located?

Answers on page 142

Photo Answers

Page 139, Top Photo: Lewis Temple (ca. 1800-1854) invented the toggle iron, the only tool to have revolutionized the whaling industry in the nineteenth century. He was a freed slave who settled in New Bedford and worked as a blacksmith.

Page 139, Bottom Photo: Bell of Remembrance in front of the New Bedford Main Library. The bell is in honor of the Armistice of November 11, 1918, the end of World War I.

Page 140, Top Photo: Captain Joshua Slocum Monument in Cooke Memorial Park Fairhaven, Massachusetts. A monument to the first person to sail around the world solo, nowhere close to where he was born, set sail, or landed.

Page 140, Bottom Photo: Fairhaven Town Hall is the town hall of Fairhaven, Massachusetts. It is located at 40 Center Street, between Walnut and William Streets, across Center Street from the Millicent Library. The brick and stone High Victorian Gothic hall was designed by Charles Brigham and built in 1892. It was given to the town by Henry Huttleston Rogers, who also made other significant contributions to the town, including the library.

Page 141, Top Photo: It was built as a dormitory for the workers at the Marconi Radio installation in Marion.

Page 141, Bottom Photo: Bird Island off the coast of Marion.

Where is this scene?

Where is this scene?

Answers on page 146

What is in the distance of this picture?

Where is this beach located?

Answers on page 146

Where and what is this statute?

Where is this Memorial located?

Answers on page 146

Photo Answers

Page 143, Top Photo: Mattapoisett Harbor

Page 143, Bottom Photo: Goosebury Island, Westport

Page 144, Top Photo: Cuttyhunk Island off the coast of Westport

Page 144, Bottom Photo: The beach at Onset

Page 145, Top Photo: Clayton Fuller of Wareham is best known locally as sculptor of Aquene, a Native American maiden, which sits on a bluff overlooking Onset Harbor. The sculpture is reputed to represent her in summer dress from approximately 1,500 years ago. The sculpture of Aquene includes two inscribed plaques, both composed by Fuller. The first states: "I am Aquene. In the language of my people, Aquene means 'Peace.' We also have enjoyed the waters of this beautiful bay. In peace, preserve and protect it for generations yet to come."

Page 145, Bottom Photo: Thomas Derosier, U.S. Army and Fall River native. He was killed in Vietnam on July 7, 1967. Sign is located in Kennedy Park in Fall River.

What is this a picture of?

Where is this play taking place?

Answers on page 150

Where is this?

Where is this gallery located?

Answers on page 150

What is this and where is it located?

What is this and where is it?

Answers on page 150

Photo Answers

Page 147, Top Photo: Wicket's Island in Onset Harbor

Page 147, Bottom Photo: Marion Art Center theater that seats 70.

Page 148, Top Photo: Westport, MA

Page 148, Bottom Photo: Marion Art Center gallery on the second floor.

Page 149, Top Photo: Border Flats Lighthouse that also is a hotel located in the middle of the Taunton River.

Page 149, Bottom Photo: Salvador's 30 ft. tall milk can was originally located in New Bedford, MA at Salvador's Ice Cream. In 1936, the giant "milk can" was moved from Fort Rodman in New Bedford to where it still stands today on Smith Neck Rd in Dartmouth.

Where is this bench?

What is this known as and where is it?

Answers on page 154

What is this and where is this?

What is this and where is it located?

Answers on page 154

What is this picture depicting?

What is the building and the Memorial in front of it?

Answers on page 154

Photo Answers

Page 151, Top Photo: The bench is located on Island Wharf overlooking Marion Harbor just to the left of the Harbormaster office.

Page 151, Bottom Photo: An Onset cottage today. Onset was developed in the 1880s as a summer camp meeting for Spiritualists. Many of the existing cottages in Onset were built as second homes for individuals from Boston, Taunton, Brockton and other northeastern cities who gathered to hear mediums communicate with the dead. While it was run by the Spiritualists, the village was known as Onset Bay Grove.

Page 152, Top Photo: This building is known as the Double Bank Building and it was built in 1831. This Greek Revival building is located at the junction of Water and William Street, and is perhaps the most impressive building in New Bedford Whaling National Historical Park.

Page 152, Bottom Photo: This is one of John Mann's murals on display at the Resiliency Preparatory School in Fall River. There are three sets of murals, each depicting a different era in Fall River's history. The first mural series contains six panels about Native American history.

Page 153, Top Photo: From Kitansett Point across Buzzards Bay to Bourne.

Page 153, Bottom Photo: The New Bedford Whaleman's Statue is located outside of the downtown New Bedford Library. It is 107 years old.

Where is this building located?

Where is this located?

Answers on page 157

What is in the distance of this photo?

What is this building?

Answers on page 157

Photo Answers

Page 155, Top Photo: Top Island Wharf sits on inner Sippican Harbor, in the heart of Marion. The sandy shoreline ramp next to the wharf offers a place for boats large and small to launch into the harbor. Boaters can purchase a wharf slip or dinghy storage to keep their boats at Island Wharf for the summer

Page 155, Bottom Photo: Bandstand next to Mattapoisett Harbor

Page 156, Top Photo: Round Hill in Dartmouth when there was a radome on it. The radome was a navigational installation put up after World War II and demolished in 2007.

Page 156, Bottom Photo: Rochester Town Hall.

Made in USA - North Chelmsford, MA
1212327_9781928758020
09.06.2022 0926